CHARTING THE VAST PACIFIC

DISCOVERY AND EXPLORATION

The Reader's Digest Association Limited,
London

CHARTING THE VAST PACIFIC

BY JOHN GILBERT

Executive Coordinators: Beppie Harrison
                          John Mason
Design Director: Guenther Radtke
Editorial: Isobel Campbell
           Jili Gormley
           Marjorie Dickens
Picture Editor: Peter Cook
Research: Ann Reading
Cartography by Geographical Projects

This edition published in the
United Kingdom and
Republic of Ireland by The
Reader's Digest Association Limited,
25 Berkeley Square, London, W1X 6AB
in association with
Aldus Books Limited, London

(R) READER'S DIGEST
is a registered trademark of The
Reader's Digest Association, Inc.
of Pleasantville, New York, U.S.A.

© 1971 Aldus Books Ltd, London
Reprinted with amendments 1980
First published in the United Kingdom
1971 by Aldus Books Ltd,
17 Conway Street, London, W.1.

Printed in Great Britain
by Hunt Barnard Web
Offset Ltd, Aylesbury

Contents

Frontispiece : Dutch seamen and traders were among the first Europeans to explore thoroughly the lands of the Pacific Ocean. Here Dutch merchant ships are seen arriving home from a voyage to the East Indies in the 1600's.

Left : the Portuguese explorer Ferdinand Magellan was the first European to sail across the vast Pacific Ocean in 1520 – 1521. It was Magellan, too, who named it *Pacific,* which means peaceful.

List of Maps

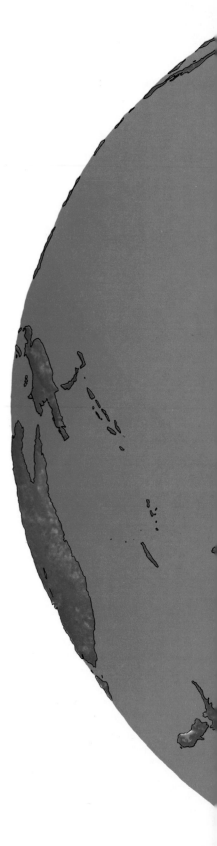

The globe illustrates the Pacific Ocean, the exploration of which this book describes. The Pacific is both the largest and deepest body of water on the earth. It covers more than a third of the earth's surface. It stretches from the frozen north to the frozen south, and its waters lap the shores of the warm islands of the tropics.

The Great South Sea
1

On September 25, 1513, the conquistador Vasco Núñez de Balboa stood on a hilltop in Darien on the east coast of the Isthmus of Panama. Gazing down on an ocean which no European had ever seen before, Balboa named it the "South Sea." Four days later, after journeying down to the coast, he waded into the waves and claimed the ocean and its islands for his master, Ferdinand II of Spain.

Balboa and his companions, setting eyes for the first time on the ocean which Magellan later called the Pacific, had no conception of its size. Their "South Sea" was the biggest expanse of water in the world, stretching westward to occupy some 64 million square miles. The islands so casually mentioned by Balboa were numbered in their thousands, and many had been populated for centuries.

Crossing the Pacific today, even by the now traditional sea routes, one can still get some idea of the ocean's vastness. One cannot fail to notice, for instance, how little land there is in relation to the miles of empty water—something generations of early voyagers must have discovered to their tragic cost. But the true extent and character of the Pacific can be properly judged only from the air.

From an airplane setting off, say, from Singapore, to cross from west to east, the initial impression will be misleading. At first there is more land than sea. The large East Indian islands of Sumatra, Java, Flores, Sumba, Borneo, Celebes, Timor, and Seram are all well-watered and forested. Heavily populated, and in places richly cultivated, they reach out like stepping-stones in the direction of New Guinea and Australia. Then, as soon as the aircraft veers north and northeastward, beyond the region of the large islands, Oceania proper begins. This part of the southern and central Pacific, three million square miles in extent, is estimated to contain more than 10,000 islands. Flying high over the islands the observer has an unimpeded view from horizon to horizon. Here the water is an unbroken sheet of blue, with not even a fleck of white to betray the presence of waves breaking over a coral strand. If the plane flies low enough, there may be a glimpse from time to time of a tiny patch of sand or shingle, a cluster of palms, and dark blotches of scrub with

Left: the men who first gazed at the Pacific had no idea of how vast the expanse of water would prove to be, nor could they imagine the thousands of islands dotted across its surface.

9

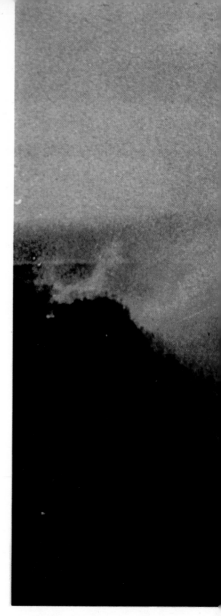

The first European to see the Pacific Ocean was Vasco Núñez de Balboa in 1513. The importance of the discovery has caught the imagination of many men, among them John Keats. Although he confused Balboa with Cortes, his famous poem "On First Looking Into Chapman's Homer," brings the moment of wonder to life:

"He star'd at the Pacific—and all his men Look'd at each other with a wild surmise. Silent, upon a peak in Darien."

no sign of human habitation. Sometimes, there may be an unexpected view of a larger island with trees, mountains, and villages. As often as not, such an island is separated from its nearest neighbor by another huge expanse of ocean.

Although the waters can be peaceful enough in glittering sunshine, sudden storms can lash the same calm waves into fury. Safe in his aircraft seat, the modern traveler can only marvel at the amazing fortitude and faith of the first Pacific voyagers in their frail canoes. What skill and good fortune, or what combination of both, could have brought them to safe landfall in such an enormous, unpredictable ocean? An ocean, moreover, unexplored and uncharted? The earliest migrants had no certainty that there was any land at all beyond the horizon. Many of them did arrive at a destination. Many more must have drifted at the mercy of waves and weather, and died.

The character and distribution of the Pacific Islands have had an important bearing on their history and settlement. Broadly speaking, the islands are divided into two groups, the volcanic islands and the coral islands, or *atolls*, to give them their geological name. The volcanic islands are the larger. Some of them have mountain ranges and volcanoes rising to 16,000 feet above sea level. Their rock structure is a dark gray to black, fine-grained rock known as basalt. Their soil is rich and well suited to mixed cultivation. Some have luxuriant vegetation, with areas of tropical rain forest and grassland, and networks of streams and rivers. Early settlers who landed on these volcanic islands were fortunate. They were able to introduce and to cultivate successfully many fruits and plants still typical today—bananas, yams, coconuts, breadfruit, pineapples, sweet potatoes, taro, and cassava. Later settlers found the soil fertile enough for sugar cane, rice, coffee, and cocoa. Despite the high

Some of the Pacific Islands are volcanic. They formed as volcanoes which erupted under the ocean, spilling layer upon layer of lava onto the seabed. The Pacific is almost completely volcano-encircled. The circle, sometimes called "the circle of fire," lies along the coast of New Zealand, running through the Philippines to Japan, across the north Pacific to the coast of North America, to South America and the world's highest volcano in Argentina.

incidence of disease, particularly malaria, generations of settlers lived and worked in these surroundings until pressures of various kinds—invasions, tribal feuds, and population explosions—drove them elsewhere.

The atolls are more typical than the volcanic islands of the romantic concept of the Pacific formed by people who have never visited it, but whose imaginations have been stirred by fiction or movies. These small coral islands are less generously endowed than the volcanic ones, and are generally less populated. They are formed from limestone that settles out from seawater and is deposited in the tissues of various marine organisms. Their encrusted skeletons gradually build up from below the ocean surface in the same way as do the great barrier reefs and continental fringing reefs, some of which are hundreds of miles in length. The reef-builders can survive only at certain depths, usually not more than 150 feet beneath the surface, and in water temperatures of roughly 68–70°F (20–21°C). The temperature requirements mean that coral reefs and islands are found mostly in tropical seas.

There are several theories as to how the atolls took their present form. Some probably sprang up from the rim of undersea volcanoes or mountains, growing bigger over the years with the addition of sand and sediment. Support for this view is given by the fact that some islands consist of little more than a circular fringe, often broken in places, enclosing a calm lagoon. The lagoon, it is supposed, covers land that has gradually subsided. Another theory disputes this, arguing that the lagoons are too shallow, and their floors are too flat, to make this interpretation acceptable.

Most atolls are small, rarely more than a few miles in diameter. They are irregular in shape, with perhaps some scrub and grass but not much soil or fresh water. Some atolls are devoid of trees, while others support a few coconut and pandanus palms which have long sword-like leaves. Sometimes, raised coral islands are found, flat slabs of limestone formed by the gradual raising of old coral reefs, with scatterings of vegetation and traces of minerals. Such islands must have been a welcome sight to mariners in olden times after weeks at sea. Many, however, could have served only as temporary resting points before the travelers pushed on in search of islands that offered more encouragement for permanent settlement.

The majority of the islands in the Pacific are grouped together

under the name Oceania. There are three major geographical groups in Oceania: Melanesia: "black islands," Micronesia: "small islands," and Polynesia: "many islands." Each of these three regions differs greatly from the other two in extent, physical characteristics, and population. Australia, Indonesia, Formosa, the Philippines, Japan, and the Kuril and Ryukya islands are not generally included as part of Oceania.

Melanesia lies to the northeast of Australia. It consists in the main of a group of large- and medium-sized volcanic islands. Among these are the large islands of New Guinea, and the islands of the Bismarck Archipelago, including New Britain and New Ireland.

Above: coral, which grows into reefs and small islands, is formed by numerous little sea animals called polyps. These animals only live in warm and tropical seas where the temperature never drops below 65 degrees. Because of the colors and shapes certain kinds of coral can be made into decorative jewelry.

Other Melanesian islands include the Louisiade Archipelago, the Solomon Islands, the Santa Cruz group, the New Hebrides, the Loyalty Islands, New Caledonia, and the Fiji group.

Micronesia, the region due east of the Philippines and to the north of Melanesia, is made up largely of atolls. These include the Gilbert and Marshall groups, and other mixed island chains such as the Mariana and the Caroline Islands, and such outposts as Nauru and Ocean Island.

Polynesia is larger than the other two areas combined. It can most easily be pictured as a huge triangle, some 5,000 miles along each side. The northernmost tip takes in the Hawaiian Islands, some of them lying just outside the tropics. In the southwest corner, well south of the tropical zone, is New Zealand. At the eastern extremity is Easter Island. Along the western edge of the triangle, fringing both Melanesia and Micronesia, lie the Tonga Islands, the islands of Samoa, the Tokelau Islands, and the Phoenix group. Straddling the equator on either side, and roughly midway between Hawaii and

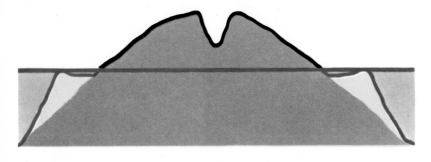

Left: how a coral island is formed Polyps gather around the base of a volcanic island and, in time, coral grows up around the sides of the volcano.

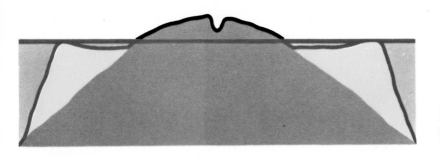

Gradually the volcano is eroded by the sea and the weather. Below the surface of the ocean the coral is growing thicker.

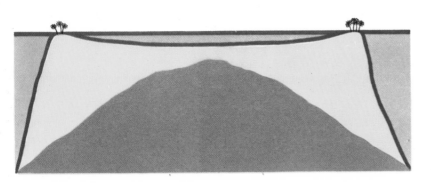

The volcanic island has been eroded so much that it is now submerged. The coral has reached the surface on either side of the volcano and also grown together across the top. The coral now forms a hollow ring on the surface with a thin covering of earth that supports vegetation. In the center, where the coral has not yet reached the surface, is a shallow pool or lagoon. With the passing of time, what was once a volcanic island has now become a coral island or atoll.

ARCTIC CIRCLE

120°

NEW SIBERIAN IS.

180°

120°

ARCTIC OCEAN

BERING STR.

A S I A

ARAL SEA

Yenisey

Lena

SEA OF OKHOTSK

SAKHALIN

BERING SEA

Alaska

Yukon

Mackenzie

HUDSON BA

N O R T H

Indus

Ganges

Hwang Ho

Yangtze R.

KURILSKIYE OST. [KURIL IS.]

SEA OF JAPAN

HOKKAIDO

Missouri

A M E R

TROPIC OF CANCER

Mekong

EAST CHINA SEA

HONSHU

KYUSHU

RYU KYU IS.

TAIWAN (FORMOSA)

ALEUTIAN IS.

MIDWAY

P A C I F I C

GULF MEXICO

BAY OF BENGAL

HAINAN

ANDAMAN IS.

SRI LANKA (CEYLON)

NICOBAR IS.

PEN. MALAYSIA

BORNEO

SOUTH CHINA SEA

PHILIPPINES

M I C R O N E S I A

MARIANA IS.

MARSHALL IS.

HAWAIIAN IS.

0° EQUATOR

SUMATRA

CELEBES

M E L A N E S I

CAROLINE IS.

BISMARCK ARCHO.

GILBERT IS.

LINE STR.

GALAPAGOS IS.

JAVA

NEW GUINEA

SOLOMON IS.

SANTA CRUZ IS.

PHOENIX IS.

TIMOR

CORAL SEA

NEW HEBRIDES

FIJI

TUVALU (ELLICE IS.)

(TUVALU)

SAMOA

MARQUESAS

TUAMOTU

O C E A N

INDIAN

TROPIC OF CAPRICORN

AUSTRALIA

NEW CALEDONIA

LOYALTY IS.

TONGA

SOCIETY IS.

COOK IS.

TAHITI

TUBUAI IS. (AUSTRAL- IS.)

PITCAIRN I

EASTER I

OCEAN

KERMADEC IS.

P O L Y N E S I A

TASMAN

NEW ZEALAND

TASMANIA

SEA

KERGUELEN IS.

120°

ANTARCTIC CIRCLE

180°

120°

© Geographical Projects

———— Polynesian Triangle

0   1000   2000   300

The world, showing the Pacific
regions of Micronesia and Melanesia.
Polynesia is the entire region
contained within the red triangle.

Tahiti, are the Line Islands. To the southeast of these lie the Marquesas
Islands. The Society Islands, including Tahiti, are almost in the dead
center of the triangle. Around them lie the islands of the Tuamotu
group and single islands such as Mangareva and Pitcairn, Rapa, the
Tubuai Islands, and the Cook Islands. Some of these are known still
by their ancient Polynesian names, others by names which date from
the European period of rediscovery.

The peoples who inhabit each area are different in many ways,
although there are overlapping resemblances. Their physical
characteristics, such as type of hair, shape of nose, and height, differ.
Their languages and dialects, their social, religious, and cultural
habits, and their traditions and folklore are individual to each group.
This diversity shows that it is unlikely they all originated from the
same race.

The questions about the present-day populations of these islands
still intrigue, perplex, and divide the experts. Where did they come
from? Who were their ancestors? How did they travel and when did
they settle? To what extent did they mingle and overlap? How did
their separate languages and cultures develop? None of the answers
is entirely satisfactory. The problems are further confused by the
numbers of migrations to and from the islands over the centuries,
obscuring, in most cases, the original pure strains.

All these factors make the Pacific a fascinating study for various
sciences. Anthropologists have opportunities for their work of
tracing the origins of different races. Archaeologists, by excavating
the remains of prehistoric and historic peoples, their homes and
possessions, can learn more of early man. Sociologists can add to
their knowledge of the development and workings of human society.
Serious students in search of the answers turn to the only reliable
evidence at their disposal. They examine the present populations and
their ways of life, their beliefs, the products they manufacture, and
all the available archaeological clues. The only point on which the
experts agree is that Oceania was the last major region, apart from
the North and South Poles, to be explored and settled by Europeans
in modern times. The main issues—the identity of the original
population, where they came from and when—are still matters for
lively argument. But the survival of Stone Age tribes and the results
of scientific dating tests indicate that the pattern of settlement in the
Pacific is more ancient and complex than was once thought.

Maoris, natives of New Zealand, belong
to the Polynesian group of Pacific
Islanders. They are above average in
height, and have light brown skin.
Many women, like this Maori, tattoo
their faces, while the men tattoo their
whole bodies.

The First Arrivals
2

Several hundred millions of years ago, long before man appeared on the planet earth, the continents now separated by oceans were probably linked together. The theory of "Continental Drift," now generally accepted, follows from the belief that one or more supercontinents existed millions of years ago. It, or they, gradually broke up, drifted apart, or the land may not have drifted but been submerged by waves and weather. When remains of *Lystrosaurus*, a three-foot-high reptile-like hippopotamus from the 195-million-year-ago Triassic era, were discovered in Antarctica some years ago, it gave powerful scientific support to the theory. The remains proved to be identical with fossil remains found in South Africa.

In very remote times, then, Asia, the East Indies, New Guinea, Australia, and New Zealand may have been very closely joined, with only short stretches of shallow water dividing the land areas. At the

It is thought that islanders used canoes similar to these, seen by Cook on one of his visits to Tahiti, when they traveled from one island to another in their earlier migrations.

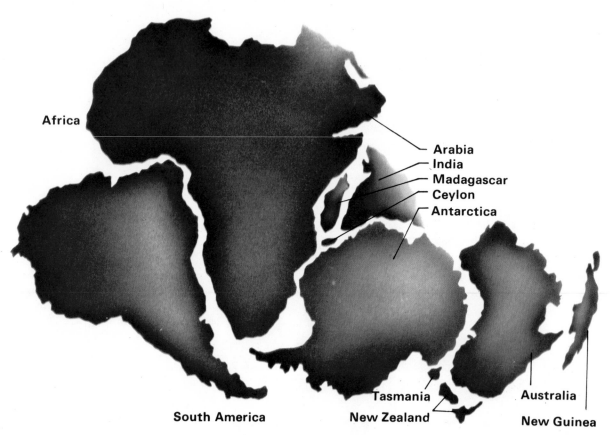

Africa

Arabia
India
Madagascar
Ceylon
Antarctica

South America

Tasmania
New Zealand

Australia
New Guinea

The Continental Drift theory, accepted by most scientists, establishes that the continents and large islands in the Southern Hemisphere fitted together into one supercontinent as did those in the Northern Hemisphere. This diagram shows how the South Pole would fit as the center of the Southern Continent.

end of the most recent Ice Age—the period which started about 2 million years ago and ended approximately 10,000 years back—the waters from the melting ice rose up to swamp many of these land bridges. Traces of the great ice sheet remain in the snowcapped peaks of the Himalaya and the continental glaciers. Many volcanic islands, too, are relics of submerged continents. Measured from the sea floor they are estimated to be as high as the Himalaya.

It seems reasonable to take the view that the very first settlers of the Pacific traveled by means of the comparatively simple island-chain route from southeast Asia. But it is clear that such conveniently arranged volcanic island masses did not exist, even 10,000 years ago, in what are now Micronesia and Polynesia. Settlement of these regions must have entailed long sea voyages.

Of the three areas under consideration, Melanesia presents fewest problems. There are many local variations, but the Melanesians are

Right: some islanders, like this New Guinea highlander, live away from European influence, and have changed little since their ancestors first arrived on the islands. They give scientists an idea of what the first islanders looked like and what their pattern of daily life might have been.

in the main dark skinned, with frizzy hair and thick lips. They resemble Negroids but are not of Negroid origin. Pictures of some of the few remaining Stone Age tribes living in the interior of New Guinea give an idea of what these first settlers of Melanesia looked like. They are similar to other ancient peoples in the Andaman Islands, the Philippines, and Malaya. Some of them have been called Negritos, distinguished from other primitive races such as the Australian Aborigines by their diminutive size. Until recently the Negritos were quite untouched by the hand of Western so-called "civilization." Having lived cut off from the influence of the Western world for many centuries they had preserved their Stone Age culture and way of life intact.

Negritos of very similar physique and appearance may have been the original inhabitants of the Melanesian islands. Pushed out of their homelands in southeastern Asia, they may have made their

way by slow stages over the separated but close land masses of the Indies to New Guinea. They may have begun their enforced migration as long as 40,000 years ago, using rafts and dugout canoes to cross the narrow strips of water. They populated the forest regions of New Guinea, and some of the neighboring islands.

The next immigrants from Asia were probably, although not certainly, the Australian Aborigines. These Australoid people probably had some resemblance to the modern Vedda people of southern India and Ceylon. The Aborigines are dark skinned with black but not wiry hair, and are not of Negroid stock. They established themselves in the northern part of the continent later known

Above: Aborigines, shown fishing in this 1819 watercolor, traveled to Australia from either the mainland of Asia or the islands of Java and Sumatra. Archaeologists have found evidence that they arrived in Australia at least 25,000 years ago.

as Australia. The Aborigines were followed, or even, some experts think, preceded by the Oceanic peoples, related to the Negritos but taller and more robustly built. The invaders succeeded in driving the pygmies into mountain and forest retreats from which they never again emerged. Although the Oceanic peoples intermingled with other racial groups they tended to remain dominant in New Guinea and the adjoining islands. Those who stayed in New Guinea became known as Papuans. Those who journeyed farther became the inhabitants of Melanesia.

Finally, in this earliest period, there were influxes of Proto-Mongoloid people, probably from northern Asia. Their modern counterparts are the Ainu, who live in Hokkaido, the northernmost island of Japan. They have dark wavy hair and extremely hairy bodies. At one time there was a theory that they were related to the Australian Aborigines.

All these different peoples were hunters, food-gatherers, and fishermen. Wherever two or more waves of immigrants converged and made their homes, original stocks were mingled with hybrid (or mixed-race) strains. The Papuan-speaking peoples gradually spread eastward across the Bismarck Archipelago and south through the Solomon and New Hebrides Islands, New Caledonia, and smaller islands to Fiji. There, perhaps having found their ideal home, they halted. There is no record of them crossing into Polynesia.

About 4,000 or 5,000 years ago, during the Neolithic era—the New Stone Age—there was another succession of migrations, from eastern Asia. Some of these followed the traditional route through

Above: each new wave of immigrants taught new skills to the Pacific Islanders. This simple gourd flask from Melanesia was easy to make with available materials. But the stone ax, although simple, was not made until new travelers taught the island's inhabitants to grind stone.

Left: the Ainu are thought by many to be one of the oldest existing peoples on earth. They live in northeastern Japan and are known best for their heavy growth of body hair. The men have bushy beards and many of the women tattoo their faces with lines which represent beards.

25

the Malay Peninsula via the East Indies into New Guinea and Melanesia. These travelers are known as Proto-Malays or Indonesians (not to be confused with the inhabitants of modern Indonesia). When they set out they were already a hybrid group, made up of Mongoloid and possibly Caucasoid strains. They did not conform to the modern idea either of yellow-skinned Mongoloids or of fair-skinned Caucasoids. The Proto-Malays were of medium height, their hair was black (in some cases wavy, in some straight), their skins were light brown and they had broad cheekbones. They brought with them much new knowledge and various skills. Among these were methods of grinding and polishing stone to make tools, utensils, and weapons. They had also acquired an ability to construct immense fortifications and monuments, and to fashion larger and more reliable boats than the earlier migrants. The Proto-Malays' way of life was based on farming rather than hunting. They carried with them from their Asian homelands roots, tubers, and seedlings of plants and fruits, and brought with them domestic animals—fowls, pigs, and dogs. When the newcomers met with the already existing populations, they either dispersed them forcibly or mixed with them. In the course of many generations the different mixed

Micronesians live in simple houses, with roofs of leaves supported by poles. During the day all four sides can be opened to catch light breezes. But at night coconut matting "blinds" are lowered to give privacy.

racial strains which resulted were again difficult to separate and distinguish. Like their predecessors, the mixed-race descendants followed sea routes to the north and east in the quest for new lands.

The scattered islands of Micronesia, to the north of Melanesia, were probably settled at about the same time as this second great wave of migration. The large islands to the west—the Philippine Islands—may have been used by groups of Proto-Malays as stepping-stones to eventual landfall in the Palau Archipelago, at the western edge of Micronesia. Others may well have arrived via the Bismarck Archipelago. In both cases such migrations were gradual processes, the move from one island group to another usually being spread over several generations.

The livelihood the settlers found on the lonely, low-lying coral islands of Micronesia was in harsh contrast to the existence they had left behind. They had come from lushly vegetated land. They settled on sparse, near-barren atolls, and their way of life accordingly had to change. As they became used to mere subsistence farming, they forgot old skills. Perhaps because they no longer had the natural raw materials, they forgot crafts they had once been practiced in, such as pottery-making and weaving. But they went on handing down other gifts from generation to generation. Among these were the techniques of boatbuilding, and skill in seafaring and the making of navigational charts (see p. 35). Thus many of the settlers continued their eastward path into the unknown sea. Passing the Mariana and the Caroline Islands, they crossed the atoll-littered sea to the Marshall and Gilbert groups. Others, less venturesome, remained at home. Their blood mingled with Melanesian blood, and with that of subsequent seafarers from Asia.

Most of the Pacific Islands are covered with dense undergrowth and forest, so thick and dark it is almost impenetrable. Narrow footpaths have to be cleared periodically to connect the various villages.

The first visitors to Easter Island saw
gigantic stone statues, topped with
red blocks to symbolize fair hair.
There are many early reports of
pale-skinned Polynesians, making the
problem of where they came from
particularly tantalizing to
anthropologists today.

The Polynesian Mystery

3

Polynesia is the largest and most complex of the Pacific regions, and the one which has caused most speculation and controversy. Except in the areas where the region overlaps in the west with Melanesia and Micronesia, the inhabitants of Polynesia show marked differences from their neighbors. Most Polynesians are tall and well-built, with massive physiques. Their skin colors are appreciably lighter, and instead of the frizzy hair typical of the true Negroid, most of them have straight or wavy hair. There are, too, examples of fair-skinned, red-haired, or bearded Polynesian men. All Polynesians, moreover, speak dialects of one recognizable language. This fact supports the view that settlement must have come from one direction, and over a relatively short period. This is in marked contrast with Micronesia, and even more so with Melanesia. In both of these groups there are many distinct languages, bearing little or no resemblance to one another.

Most experts believe that Polynesia was the last of the Pacific areas to be settled. Others hold that it must have been the first. All agree that the earliest settlers came originally from Asia. And all deduce that because Polynesians do not show typical Negroid or Mongoloid features they must, by process of elimination, have some Caucasoid blood. The unsolved mystery is whether they came by the same routes as the Melanesians and Micronesians, traveling steadily eastward, or whether they found their way in the first place to the Americas and then struck out westward. Both theories have much to commend them, but both have flaws.

The "traditional" theory, held by most anthropologists and sociologists, suggests that at some time during the New Stone Age settlers infiltrated into Polynesia from the west. They may have come by either the Melanesian or the Micronesian route, or possibly both. Peoples of pygmy stock may have been among them, for there are traditions in Hawaii, the Society Islands, the Marquesas Islands, and New Zealand of dwarf-like people known as Menahunes or Manahunes, who were vanquished by later arrivals. Logic demands that the settlers would have made their first stops in those island groups nearest to them: Samoa, Tonga, and, if they traveled by Micronesia, Hawaii. Doubtless they brought with them plants, fruits, and animals from their home islands. In time, again by gradual stages over 1,500 or 2,000 years, they would have penetrated to the heart of Polynesia. They were more advanced culturally and tech-

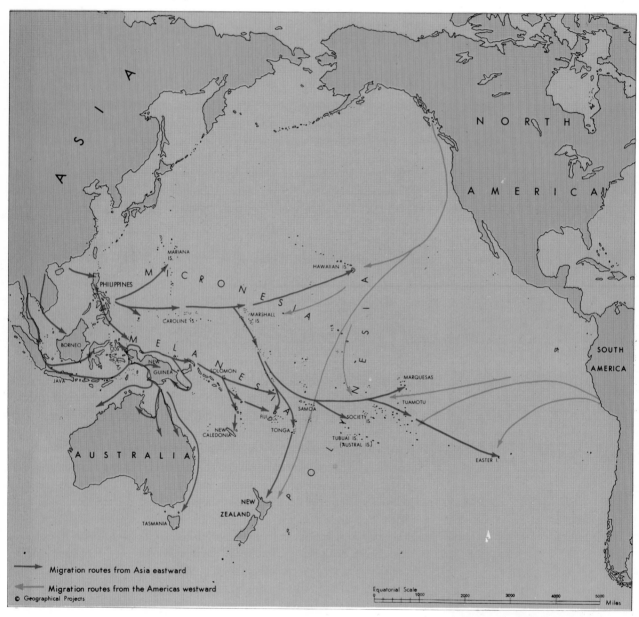

ASIA

NORTH
AMERICA

MARIANA
IS.

PHILIPPINES

M I C R O N E S I A

HAWAIIAN IS.

CAROLINE IS.

MARSHALL
IS.

BORNEO

MELANESIA

NEW
GUINEA

JAVA

SOLOMON
IS.

FIJI

NEW
CALEDONIA

TONGA

SAMOA

P O L Y N E S I A

MARQUESAS

TUAMOTU

SOCIETY
IS.

TUBUAI IS.
(AUSTRAL IS.)

SOUTH
AMERICA

EASTER I.

AUSTRALIA

TASMANIA

NEW
ZEALAND

→ Migration routes from Asia eastward

→ Migration routes from the Americas westward

© Geographical Projects

Equatorial Scale

0   1000   2000   3000   4000   5000

Miles

How the people came to the islands
of the Pacific. Some migrated
there from Asia (the routes shown
in red) and others from the Americas
(the routes shown in blue).

nically than the Negritos, perhaps because they were of Proto-Malayan stock. Like the inhabitants of the western Caroline Islands, they must have been hardy seafarers accustomed to long ocean journeys.

The myths and traditions of the Pacific Islands are rich in tales of gods, demi-gods, leaders, and heroes who sailed from an ancestral homeland and then fanned out in different directions. It is impossible to treat the legends as history, for there are many inconsistencies. But there are enough significant common features to construct a feasible theory with a chronological sequence of events. At some time during the Christian era, perhaps as late as the 1100's to 1300's, descendants of the sea god Tangaroa sailed from a homeland variously known, according to local dialects, as Hawaiki (the Maori name), Havai'i (the Society Islands name), Savai'i (the Samoan name), or simply Hawai'i. The similarities of language and tradition clearly indicate a composite group which populated the island outposts of Polynesia without encountering other racial groups on the way. But because of the Polynesian habit of naming new lands after older ones, the identification of this ancestral homeland is pure guesswork. It may have been Savaii, the largest island in the Samoan group. It may have been Raiatea in the Society Islands. It may even have been Hawaii itself.

Whether they came by a northern or southern route the travelers would at some point have reached Samoa, Tonga, and the islands to the north. Those fortunate enough to have survived the arduous sea journey would have found the new islands pleasant, and the climate bearable and free of the dread disease we know as malaria. From Tonga and Samoa they would in time have established trade links with Melanesian Fiji, and developed a regular two-way exchange of goods.

The bolder souls are then assumed to have pushed farther on to the heartlands of Polynesia, to the lush volcanic group later known as the Society Islands. Here, on the island of Raiatea (not on its larger neighbor Tahiti), they set up an important religious and cultural center, probably before A.D. 500. On this and adjoining islands, the settlers erected large stone altars and there they worshiped their gods. The society evolved as a closely knit community whose leaders were the senior members of the largest families and the priests. Many forms of tabu were practiced. The word

Left: islanders became skilled at using the natural materials they found on the islands they reached. This tapa cloth from Samoa was made by first soaking the inner bark of a tree in shallow water for a few days. Then the wet bark was laid on a smooth stone and beaten with a special wooden mallet. This caused the bark to become a thin, stiff, porous paper, which was thickened by beating several sheets together.

Below : Polynesians worshiped their ancestors before explorers arrived and taught them Christianity. The island of Raiatea was a religious center for the islanders, and numerous stone altars were erected, like this one called the Marae of Tapu Tapu Atea.

"tabu" or "taboo" or "tapu" is of Polynesian origin. Literally the word means "marked off." It implies that certain people or things are unsafe for casual contact, either because they are sacred or because they are unclean. Gods were invoked to bless any enterprise or journey. In some places human sacrifices were offered. Where timber was plentiful, wood carving and decoration were of a high standard. The Polynesians built stout houses and seaworthy boats, and made ingenious use of earth, wood, and stone for implements and utensils, and of skins and vegetable fibers for clothes. Their methods of cultivation as well as their skill in hunting and fishing allowed them to enjoy a reasonable standard of living.

After many generations, these fearless mariners set off to find other islands, reaching a peak of activity between the 1100's and 1800's. Some of the discoveries they made were doubtless accidental. Others were the results of well organized colonizing expeditions. Men, women, children, and animals, with plentiful stocks of food and water, and an assortment of plants, embarked in outrigger canoes on voyages that might last weeks or months. Their pioneering voyages must have been do-or-die ventures. Even with intervening resting points, the distances covered were considerable—hundreds, even thousands, of miles. Long journeys, south to the Tubuai Islands and New Zealand, north to Hawaii, and east to Mangareva and Easter Island, could hardly have been anything but one-way voyages.

What of the boats in which these intrepid explorers set out to brave the unknown? All available evidence shows that the Polynesians were accomplished boatbuilders. Basically their vessels consisted of various kinds of dugout canoes. Some were fairly small, obviously designed for fishing and local trade. Others were larger,

Above: boats were very important to islanders as their only means of travel, and fishing was one of their main food sources. Even now canoes are made in the traditional way, but now with better tools.

Above: this small stone sculpture is a model of the reed boats that islanders might have used to sail to Easter Island. Canoes of this kind were seen by the Spanish off the coast of Peru in the early 1500's.

stronger, and better adapted to the rough waters encountered on longer voyages. The hulls were fashioned from single trunks or from shorter lengths of plank. And the craftsmen worked with tools made from whatever local materials were available—cutting tools made of stone, coral, or fishbone. The sides of the canoe were built up to afford extra strength and protection. For this purpose the planks were sewn together with strands of vegetable fiber, usually coconut husks, threaded through holes bored in the wood. To make the completed hull watertight, the crevices were stuffed with mixtures of earth and charcoal or vegetable gum. Finally the canoe was painted in various colors and decorated as required.

Different methods were used to stabilize the canoe in the water. In some canoes a thin strut of wood was fixed parallel to the hull, connected by wooden booms to the *gunwales* (sides of the canoe). An even more effective stabilizer was made by lashing a second canoe alongside, joined to the first by booms and serving as a balance— the original catamaran. These stabilizers were termed *outriggers*. It was possible to erect a plank deck and an elementary cabin super-structure over the double canoe. The canoes were moved in two ways. They could be paddled by oars, in which case a large steering paddle served as the rudder, or they could be sailed with a triangular lateen sail. Standard equipment also included anchors and bailers. Such canoes measured anything from 60 to 100 feet in length. They could provide adequate space and the necessities of life such as food and water for up to 100 people or more on a voyage lasting several weeks.

The European explorers found these canoes both fast and sea-worthy. Captain Cook saw both types, including the single *flying proa*—no relation of the modern Malayan vessel of the same name. The Maori war canoes that he encountered were of a different type, without outriggers.

These canoes might have been seaworthy, but they must have

been risky too. In rough seas they must have leaked badly, and no doubt many capsized despite all the efforts of the crew and the prayers of the priests on board.

The amazing fact is that somehow the Polynesians managed to navigate their frail craft across hundreds of miles of empty ocean. The distances involved were enormous. The Hawaiian Islands are at least 1,800 miles from the nearest Micronesian islands. Fiji is some 500 miles from the nearest Melanesian land. Yet somehow the Polynesians crossed these expanses of open sea. Their only guides were natural ones: the sun, the clouds, the moon and stars, the waves and winds, and the flights of migratory birds. But where there was no certainty of land ahead, and no glimpse of a friendly coastline in any direction, the Polynesians had to rely exclusively on experience, observation, common sense, and luck.

By day they could learn something from the position of the sun, provided it shone, by night from the stars, when they were not obscured by clouds. They must have had some knowledge, too, of prevailing winds and currents, and could have learned something from the direction of surface waves. But over long distances, and with so many local variations, wind and water would not provide foolproof guides. Storms and natural drift, especially on overcast

Above: everything on the small islands was put to as many uses as possible. The fruit of the pandanus tree was eaten. The fibers of the same tree were used in weaving and made into sails and "paper" for maps.

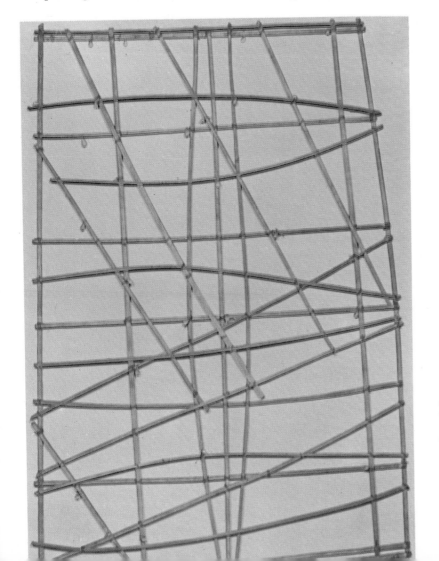

Left: the Micronesians were skilled sailors and navigators. For frequent, two-way journeys, they made navigation charts like this, with small stones or shells indicating islands and sticks to show the routes and ocean currents.

35

Below: outrigger canoes were unknown in New Zealand when explorers first landed there. But in other parts of Polynesia, where this model was made they were the common transportation.

nights, must have thrown countless vessels far off course. With calm, clear weather, it was feasible to sail along a given latitude. But to fix a longitudinal bearing with any degree of accuracy must have been beyond even the Polynesians' navigational skill. On known routes, and on the return passage of a two-way voyage, distinctive landmarks could be utilized. It is hard, however, to disagree with those who say that, even granting their considerable navigational abilities, many of the earliest discoveries of the Polynesians were due to luck and accident rather than judgment. The later Europeans, even with their elaborate navigational aids, often found themselves helplessly lost in these vast expanses of ocean.

The problems of navigation have prompted some people to wonder whether the entire theory of west-east movement of population should be revised. The Norwegian ethnologist Thor Heyerdahl, one of several to think so, has marshaled a large body of evidence to support an opposing theory, backed up by personal experiment.

Heyerdahl pointed out, in the first place, that any migrations from west to east would have been quite contrary to all the main systems of prevailing winds and currents. Was it not more probable therefore

Above: *Kon-Tiki*, the raft in which Norwegian ethnologist Thor Heyerdahl and five companions drifted about 4,100 miles westward across the Pacific Ocean from Peru in 1947. The expedition aimed to prove that South American Indians could have sailed to Polynesia. Here *Kon-Tiki* is seen approaching the coast of one of the Tuamotu Islands in the central Pacific at the end of its epic voyage.

Left: Thor Heyerdahl (left) talking to the Swedish historian Bjørn Landström. The controversial voyage of the *Kon-tiki* caused world-wide interest and excitement at the time.

that Polynesia was settled from the other direction, from the continent later known as America, and that the migrants had two main starting points, one the west coast of South America, the other the northwest coast of North America?

There are many arguments in favor of such a theory, not the least of them sheer logic. After all, most of the European voyages of discovery—Spanish, Dutch, British, and French—took the routes from east to west. Their ships followed the southeast trade winds and south equatorial current in the Southern Hemisphere, and the northeast trades and north equatorial current in the Northern Hemisphere. Supporters of the traditional theory argue that, despite the difficulties of sailing against wind and current, the Polynesians could have achieved their long voyages by taking advantage of the summer westerlies, brief and unpredictable though they were. They grant that Polynesians may have visited America and returned home, but maintain that such journeys were few and far between, and probably accidental.

The "current and wind" theory has been put to practical test in this century, both by Heyerdahl himself and by Eric de Bisschop.

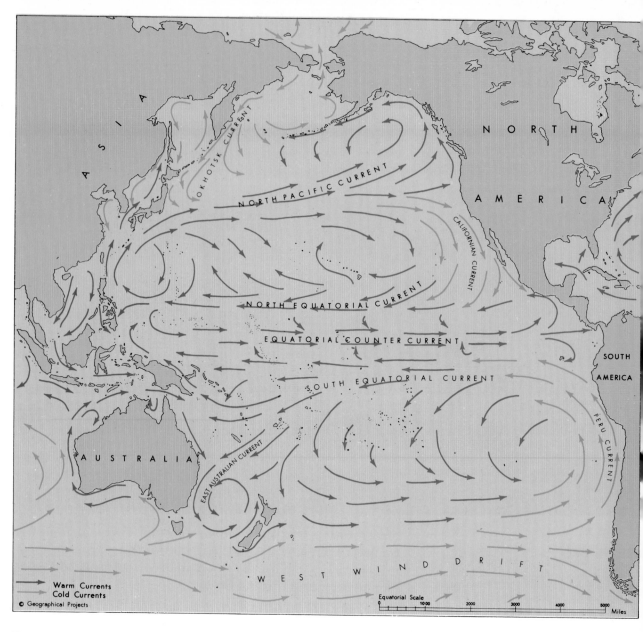

The currents of the Pacific Ocean. These great ocean currents move clockwise in the Northern Hemisphere and counterclockwise in the Southern.

Heyerdahl made a celebrated drift voyage in a balsa-wood raft, *Kon-Tiki*, which took him and his companions 4,100 miles in 101 days, from Callao in Peru to the Tuamotu Islands. De Bisschop set out to prove his own theory that Polynesians from the east could have sailed to and from Hawaii in the north, and to and from New Zealand in the south. In a modern version of a double canoe he allowed himself to be blown by trade winds from Hawaii to Java. Later De Bisschop tested the raft theory favored by Heyerdahl, attempting a voyage from Peru to Tahiti and back, but he was carried too far north, was wrecked, and died from his injuries. Significantly, he had been unable to make any progress in a west-east direction.

Some of Heyerdahl's critics have tended to dismiss his propositions out of hand, refusing to do him the justice of recognizing his claim to be a serious scientist and not a mere adventurer. His more serious opponents, who have examined the very detailed theories which formed the background to the *Kon-Tiki* expedition, point out flaws in some of the "evidence" he presents. But his evidence is by no means based solely on winds and currents. Heyerdahl argues that the whole chronological order of events put forward by earlier authorities is at fault. He does not deny that the original settlers came at one time from Asia. He suggests, however, that they

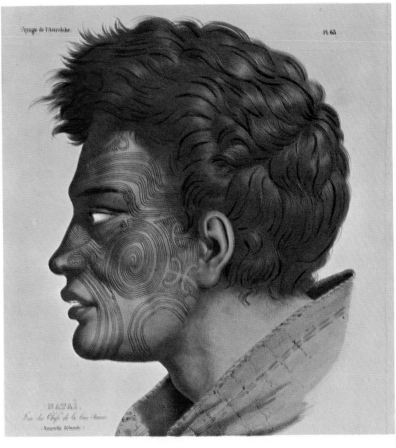

traveled by a much more northerly and less difficult route, from the eastern extremity of Asia to the western tip of America, by way of what is now called the Bering Strait and the Aleutian Island chain to the south. This is recognized by anthropologists as having provided the most likely route for North American Indians from Asia, and there were subsequent migrations down the west coast into Central and South America. Heyerdahl believes that Hawaii was reached from the northwest coast of North America after the original Asian migrants had spent many centuries in its warm and favorable climatic conditions. In separate migrations, he suggests, Easter Island, Mangareva, and the Marquesas Islands were reached by Indians from pre-Inca Peru.

In support of this double theory, Heyerdahl produces a fasci-

This drawing of a Maori chief done in 1883, shows many of the features that Thor Heyerdahl claims are similar to those of the Kwakiutl tribe of North America; light skin, dark, wavy hair, and prominent cheek bones.

nating and impressive array of accumulated evidence. He cites a number of parallels between the Polynesians, especially the Maoris, on the one hand and the Inca and northwest Indians, particularly the Kwakiutl tribe, on the other. He points, for instance, to similarities in their physical appearances. Among the many details he notes are stature, skin color, bone structure, blood groups, head shape, and hair texture. Heyerdahl also mentions the interestingly parallel styles of religious worship, particularly of the sun-god. The structures of altars and temples, and of statues, especially the extraordinary stone images on Easter Island, are remarkably alike in both areas. Heyerdahl mentions gaps in Polynesian culture that are characteristic of the people of North America but not of Melanesian or Micronesian culture. At the time the white men arrived in Polynesia, there was no trace of pottery, loomweaving, of any form of currency, or of the arch and the wheel. None of these is found among the North American Indians, either. Heyerdahl looks at the undoubted South American origin of the sweet potato widely found in Polynesia, as well as at several other kinds of plants. Finally, Heyerdahl produces evidence of the many similarities throughout the Polynesian islands in rituals, myths, and traditions. Notable among these are tales relating to the legendary hero-god Con Tici, who, in the pre-Inca period, sailed westward from South America with his Viracocha people in search of unknown lands. In many Pacific islands, Ti'i or Tiki is revered as the first man.

Modern scientific methods of dating by means of radiocarbon tests (measuring the radioactive carbon in remains of living organisms) have also convinced Heyerdahl and his school that settlement of eastern Polynesia occurred far earlier—perhaps by a thousand years—than used to be generally believed. The dates, which are accepted by objective scientists, would seem to bear Heyerdahl out. There are traces of human settlement in the Marquesas Islands going as far back as 120 B.C., in Samoa from between A.D. 9 and 79, in Hawaii from around A.D. 124, and in Easter Island (allegedly the last island to be settled, at some time after A.D. 1200) between A.D. 360 and 386. According to Heyerdahl, this upsets the previous theories.

The migrants traveled, Heyerdahl claims, in canoes. These were either of the single outrigger type or the simple Indian/Maori dugout. In the case of the pre-Inca Indians, they were rafts. Balsa rafts, equipped with a sail and an ingenious set of maneuverable centerboards set between the logs, would have been both speedy and easily adapted to sail with and against the wind.

Supporters of the traditional theory allege that Heyerdahl has, for the purposes of his own argument, ignored the many resemblances between the Polynesians and their Melanesian and Micronesian neighbors, especially the language links. They are not to be shaken in their conviction that all migrations took place in a west-east direction. And there the matter rests. There is much to compel agreement, and much to sow doubt in both camps.

This nephrite tiki from New Zealand is a good luck ancestor figure. After death it was thought that men were promoted to gods, protecting spirits for their descendants. They were represented by images in which they were said to live at certain times.

Explorers and immigrants through the centuries have had a common custom of naming newly-discovered land after that which they left behind. The early islanders were no exception. Many of the Polynesian names are identical with or closely related to place names in the Tiahuanaco territory of aboriginal Peru. This list of examples shows the place names of the old Inca Empire on the left and the aboriginal place names in the Polynesian islands on the right.

INCA	POLYNESIAN
ACARI	AKARI
ACHIRI and TAQUIRI	TAHIRI
APLAO	ALAO
APURIMAC	APOLIMA
ARAPA	RAPA
ARICA	KARIKA
ATICO	ATITU
CALAMA	KALAMA
CALANA	KALANA
CAMANA	TAMANA
CAPIA	APIA
COROCORO	KORO
CORACORA	PORAPORA
HUARA	HUARA-RAI
HUATA	TAHUATA
KEA	KEA
KEA-KEA	TEA-TEA
KILI	KILI
KONA	KONA
LAMPA	RAMA
LARO	RARO
LOA	LOA
LOCUMBA	ROTUMA
MACA	MAKA
MACUSANI	MAKURANGI
MALA	MALA
MATACANE	MATAKANA
MATARANI	MATA-KITE-RANGI
MAURI	MAUI
MOCOMOCO	MOKO
OROYA	OROUA
PAKAYA	WAKAIA
PANGO	PANGOPANGO
PISCO	PIKO
POTOPOTO	POTO
PUNA	PUNA
ROMA	ROMAROMA
SICUANI	HIKURANGI
TAIPI	TAIPI
TANGA	TANGA
TARACA	TARAKA
TARAPOTO	TAKAPOTO
TARAPACA	TARAPAKU

Rediscovery

4

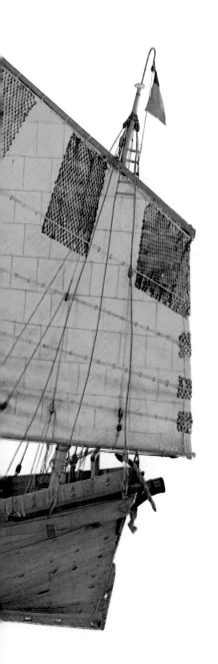

While the early Melanesian and Polynesian migrations were going on, one other seafaring people, the Chinese, were also active in the Pacific. China was far ahead of its European contemporaries in the arts of shipbuilding, mapmaking, and astronomy, as in many other fields. Although records are sparse, it is probable that Chinese merchants were trading by land and sea with India and the Persian Gulf, Malaya and the East Indies, early in the Christian era. During the Sung dynasty (A.D. 960–1279) the Chinese were responsible for many innovations which were later adopted by European navigators. They invented the magnetic compass, the sternpost rudder, and the watertight compartment. The Chinese also produced the world's first printed maps. And there is evidence to show that from the 600's onward Chinese ships were already visiting the Caroline Islands and the Philippines on trading ventures.

During the reign of the Emperor Yung Lo (1403–1424) the admiral Cheng Ho undertook a series of expeditions designed to extend Chinese influence in the Indian Ocean and South Sea. His ships used charts with proper compass bearings. These were more accurate than the charts drawn on stretched sheepskin—the *portolano* charts—prepared by European cartographers. Although Cheng Ho's ships concentrated mainly on the east coast of Africa, the Persian Gulf, and the coasts of India, we know from engravings on *steles* (monu-

Left: the Chinese were more advanced than Europeans in shipbuilding and navigation in the early 1400's. In their ocean-going junks they were trading with people in India and the Persian Gulf. They are known to have landed on several of the larger Pacific Islands, and it is thought that they visited many of the smaller islands to trade.

Right: the Chinese invented the magnetic compass and compasses like this were used until the 1800's. Note that it has only 24 points, unlike modern compasses with 32.

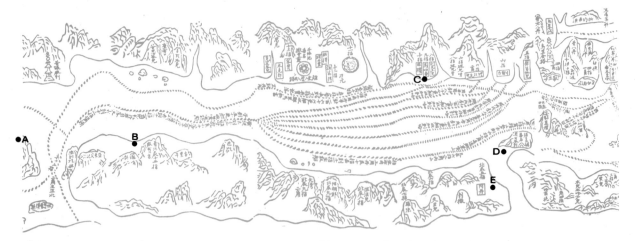

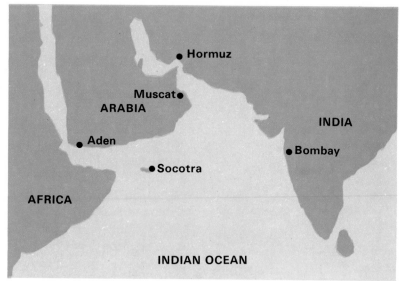

Above : Chinese sea chart drawn after the expedition of Cheng Ho in the early 1400's and printed in 1621. It shows India (top) and Arabia and Africa (bottom) separated by a rather narrow Indian Ocean. Some of the ports shown on the chart are also indicated on the modern map (right) and are keyed below :

A : Hormuz
B : Muscat
C : Bombay
D : Socotra
E : Aden

mental pillars) that at least one expedition touched land at Java and Sumatra. It is clear that the Chinese were familiar with wide areas of the North Pacific long before the Europeans arrived.

The expeditions of Cheng Ho in the 1400's coincided with the dawn of the great age of discovery, initiated by the two great naval powers of Europe, Spain and Portugal. The Spaniards sailed across the Atlantic to the New World. The Portuguese sailed around the tip of Africa to India and the Spice Islands. For both nations the motivating factors were mainly political and commercial. In Spain's case, these were reinforced by religious enthusiasm, in Portugal's by a genuine spirit of adventure and inquiry.

Mapmakers from Ptolemy (A.D. 100's) onward had provided sketchy, inaccurate, but highly alluring information about the fabulous lands of Africa, India, and the Far East. European appetites were further whetted by travelers' tales, such as those of the Venetian Marco Polo, who in the 1200's served at the court of Kublai Khan in Peking. Marco Polo brought back glowing accounts of the boundless riches of Cathay (China) and Cipango (Japan). He also told of some vague lands to the south which he called Locac and Malaiur. Polo's colorful descriptions of the potential wealth of the Orient led to a steady increase in trade between Europe and Asia. The truth of his reports then seemed to be confirmed by the goods brought back by merchants and by the stories they in turn related.

It was the Arabs, however, placed geographically astride the main land and sea routes of the time, who monopolized eastern trade. To Spain in particular, the threat of the Moors and the rapid spread of Islam (the name given to the Moslem religion) seemed

Below: typical Arab camel caravan. The Arabs, who were in a strong geographical position, had dominated the trade from the east for centuries. It was partly to gain control of this lucrative trade, and partly to outflank Islam, that Portugal and Spain searched for a new way to the east.

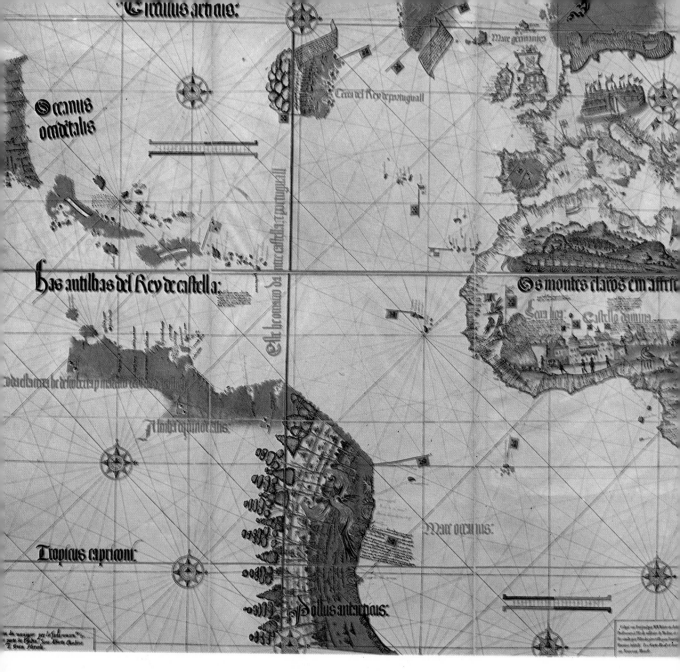

Cantino's world map, published in 1502, shows the line of demarcation agreed upon by the kings of Spain and Portugal in the Treaty of Tordesillas in 1494. The flags of both of the countries are shown flying over their colonies. Spain kept the possessions she had discovered before the treaty.

increasingly menacing. The threat had been a vital governing factor in Spanish foreign policy since the time of the Crusades. Thus the Moslem capture of Constantinople in 1453 and the collapse of the Byzantine empire came as a brutal shock. Although the Moors had played an influential part in Spanish life and affairs for 700 years, they had been kept in check. Now, with Islam extending its empire westward along the coast of North Africa and standing poised at the eastern gates to Europe, Christianity seemed endangered as never before. In the determination of Spain, and to a lesser extent Portugal, to wrest away some of the lucrative trade of the Orient from the Arab world, there was an echo of the old crusading zeal. So the year 1492 marked a double triumph for Spanish policy abroad and at home. Not only did Christopher Columbus enable Spain to secure a foothold in the New World, but the capture of the Moorish kingdom of Granada resulted in the country being united for the first time under Christian rule.-

The spirit of the Renaissance—the quest for knowledge and the belief that man stood at the center of the universe and was master of his own fate—also played a part in expanding the geographical horizons. It was best typified in the person of Portugal's Prince Henry the Navigator. His sailors discovered the Azores in the North Atlantic and pushed down the coast of Africa to the mouth of the Congo. Spain, meanwhile, set her sights on a western route to the Indies. Initially, her only success was the settlement of the Canary Islands, off the northwest coast of Africa. It was inevitable that Spain and Portugal should clash, and the naval war which ensued between them was eventually ended by a succession of treaties, laying down precisely their respective spheres of influence. In 1493, the two countries asked Pope Alexander VI to decide on a line of demarcation. The line ran from north to south about 340 miles west of the Azores and Cape Verde Islands. Spain could claim land west of the line and Portugal could claim land to the east. Dissatisfied with the Pope's ruling, Spain and Portugal drew up the Treaty of Tordesillas in 1494. They agreed that the line of demarcation was to run from Greenland to the mouth of the Amazon. The treaty confirmed Portugal's claim to Africa and to the invaluable sea route to India. As it turned out, it also gave Portugal the right to explore the coast of Brazil. The Portuguese were well satisfied with an arrangement which left Spain to colonize lands which might not even exist. After Prince Henry's death the Portuguese explorer Vasco da Gama sailed around the southern tip of Africa and reached India. His successors later opened the way to the Moluccas (the Spice Islands) and established a commercial empire in the East.

But the Treaty of Tordesillas proved less of a disadvantage to Spain than was first believed. The conquistadors who followed Columbus were to find riches enough in the new continent of America: gold and silver in Mexico, timber, dyes, spices, tobacco, cocoa, and other natural products, both on the mainland and in the West Indies.

One of the early Spanish colonists was Vasco Núñez de Balboa, a swashbuckling adventurer with a gift for leadership. He had attempted to set himself up as a farmer on the Spanish island of Hispaniola (what is now Haiti and the Dominican Republic) but had been forced to flee his creditors. Legend says he hid in a barrel of pork being loaded onto a ship and found refuge in the new colony of San Sebastian on the Colombian coast. From there he took with him a small band of people and founded the colony of Darien on the Isthmus of Panama. By a combination of negotiation, bribery, and force he won the cooperation of local Indian tribes and set his colony on a sound economic footing. The Indians hinted to Balboa of the gold to be found somewhere beyond the mountains and of the

Vasco Núñez de Balboa (1475–1519) followed directions from Indians who told of an unending sea, and found the Pacific. Over the years his success and popularity made him the target of a political rival's jealousy and false charges of treason were leveled against him. Finally in 1519 the man who had made one of the most important discoveries in history was executed in a public square.

Left: this colonial Spanish cathedral is part of the city of Panamá, important as the starting point for Spanish expeditions in search of gold, silver, and other treasure. The city was founded in 1519 on the site of an Indian fishing village. The name Panamá comes from the Indian word for "fisherman" or "plenty of fish."

"other sea" that could be reached by marching westward. Balboa was intrigued by both prospects. North and South America might yet prove to be separate. That much hoped-for goal, a western route to the Indies, might still be a possibility.

Aware that his enemies at home were exerting pressure to have him replaced as governor, Balboa lost no time in organizing an expedition of 190 Spaniards and some 800 Indian porters. The journey through the forests and over the mountains took three arduous weeks, but on September 25, 1513, Balboa was rewarded by the sight, in the far distance, of a seemingly endless expanse of ocean. A few days later he reached the coast and bathed his feet for the first time in what he assumed to be the "South Sea." All the undiscovered lands in it and all the shores lapped by its waters were promptly claimed for the Spanish crown. Three months later he returned in triumph to Darien with his exciting tidings.

But Balboa's success proved to be double-edged. Although King Ferdinand II promoted him to *adelantado* (the Spanish title for governor) of the South Sea, he was replaced as governor in Darien. The man who took over from him was one of the most inhuman of all conquistadors, the elderly Pedro Arias de Avila, who was also known as Pedrarias Dávila. All further advancement for Balboa was blocked. Even his engagement to one of Pedrarias' daughters was no help to him. In 1519, Pedrarias founded the city of Panamá on the Pacific side of the isthmus. In the same year he disposed of his enemy Balboa. Balboa was arrested on a fabricated treason charge and executed. Such was the reward of the man who had claimed the Pacific for Spain.

The news of Balboa's discovery of the Pacific delighted Spain and alarmed Portugal. An expedition in 1501, with the Florentine Amerigo Vespucci on board, had sailed down the east coast of Brazil (as was Portugal's right) and back up the west coast of Africa. The expedition proved that a great land barrier existed between

Below: Amerigo Vespucci (1451–1512) claimed he discovered a new continent for Spain in 1497. Although his name (as America) became identified with the New World, later historians gave the honor of discovery to Columbus.

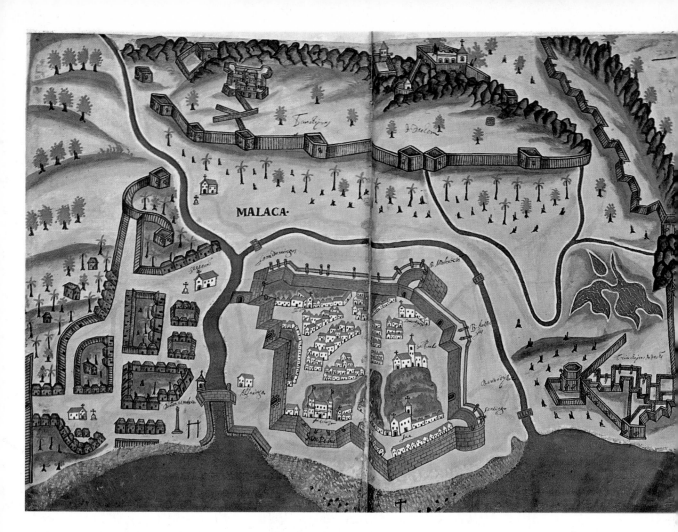

MALACA.

This painting shows Malacca after it had become a Portuguese colony. The position of the settlement, on the southwest coast of the Malay peninsula, made it an important port for the expeditions that went out looking for the "Spice Islands" and other new sources of eastern luxuries.

Europe and the Indies. There remained the possibility that the barrier could be bypassed. In 1511, Portugal had broken the Arab trading monopoly in the East by capturing Malacca, on the southwest of the Malay peninsula, and establishing itself in the Moluccas two years later. In 1514, Pope Leo X was persuaded to amend the Treaty of Tordesillas by awarding to Portugal any new lands it might discover by sailing east. Now, more than ever, Spain was impelled to pursue the quest for a practical route in the west. Ironically, it was to be a Portuguese seaman in the service of Spain who found it.

Fernão de Magalhães, or to give him his anglicized name, Ferdinand Magellan, had already served under the founder of the Portuguese empire in the East, the governor Afonso de Albuquerque. Although he had not visited the Spice Islands he knew of their existence. What neither he nor anyone else could yet determine was exactly where they lay in relation to the New World and to which nation they rightfully belonged. Magellan offered his services on several occasions to King Manuel I of Portugal. After being repeatedly spurned, Magellan turned to Spain, renouncing his nationality. From King Charles I—later the Holy Roman Emperor Charles V—he eventually obtained backing for an expedition to the

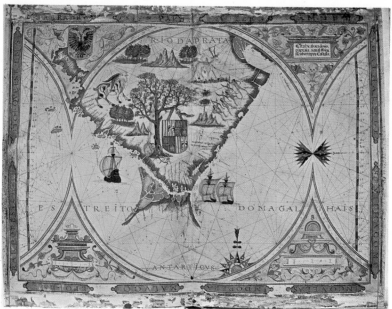

Left: this map, drawn soon after Magellan discovered the way from the Atlantic Ocean to the Pacific in 1520, shows the early misconception of the route as a clear, open passage. In fact, the real Strait of Magellan is a series of narrow, twisting channels between the islands and the tip of the South American continent.

South Sea, by way of a passage through or around the American continent. He sailed on September 20, 1519, with five small, antiquated ships. His own flagship, the *Trinidad*, was only 110 tons. The fleet's crew numbered 234 men, including one Englishman, Master Andrew of Bristol.

A firsthand account of Magellan's historic voyage is still in existence. This is the detailed diary kept on the journey by an Italian named Antonio Pigafetta who sailed with the fleet. The first part of the expedition, down the African coast and across to South America, then southward along the unexplored shores of

Uruguay and Argentina, took a full year. While anchored in the bay of San Julián, Magellan had to deal in drastic fashion with a mutiny. The *Santiago* was wrecked, the *San Antonio* deserted. On October 21, 1520 Magellan rounded the southern tip of Patagonia. He named it Cape of the Eleven Thousand Virgins. Then he named the land which stretched away farther south Tierra del Fuego, after sighting fires lit by the inhabitants on its shore. Then followed the dramatic 38-day passage through the strait between the mainland and the island to the south. On November 28, the three surviving ships broke out of the perilous strait—to be named the Strait of Magellan—into the South Sea. The point at which the open sea was first sighted was named Cape Deseado (from the Italian word for desire). They named it "as a thing," says Pigafetta, "which had been much desired for a long time." The sea itself Magellan named Mar Pacifico (the peaceful sea).

For three months Magellan experienced excellent weather conditions and was able to follow the course that he predetermined. But the placidity of the new ocean was misleading. There were many terrors and alarms in store for Magellan and his ships. Driven by

Below: Magellan's men reported the strange phenomenon of flying fish, which led European artists to create imaginary pictures of schools of fish leaping through the ships' rigging.

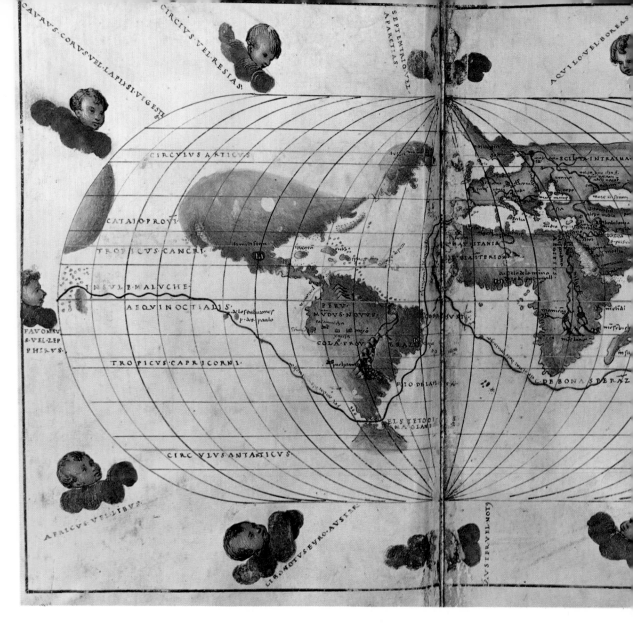

CIRCVLVS ARTICVS

CATAIO·PROVI·

TROPICVS·CANCRI·

INSVLE·MALVCHE·

AEQVINOCTIALIS·

FAVONI V
S·VEL·ZEP
HIRVS·

TROPICVS·CAPRICORNI·

CIRCVLVS ANTARTICVS·

AFRICVS·VEL·LIBVS·

LIBONOTVS·EVRO·AVSTER·

AVSTER·VEL·NOT)

the trade winds and the current, the crews despaired of ever sighting land again. For eight terrible weeks they sailed to the northwest. The heat was blistering, the meat turned rotten, the water went foul. Scurvy, the traditional scourge of seamen, began to take its toll. Soon the crew were reduced to eating "old biscuit reduced to powder and full of grubs." They "drank water that was yellow and stinking .... We ate the ox-hides from under the yardarms, also the sawdust of wood, and rats, which cost half a crown each .... The worst misfortune was that the gums of our men grew so much that they could not eat, and nineteen died." At last, on St. Paul's Day, January 24, 1521, they sighted a small coral island. The island had green vegetation but was uninhabited. There was no fresh water, but the numerous sea birds provided both meat and eggs for the famished crews. On February 3, they were able to catch some sharks off another atoll which Magellan marked in his chart as Shark's Island. The two

This map of the world shows the route taken by Magellan and his expedition. Notice the incomplete outlines of the Americas which had been discovered 30 years before Magellan's voyage, and the absence of Australia and New Zealand, which (like most of the islands of the Pacific) were still unknown to Europeans.

islands were probably Pukapuka in the Tuamotu Islands and Caroline Island, one of the Line Islands.

After passing Shark's Island and still hopeful that the Indies were within sailing distance, Magellan set a course northwest and then due west after crossing the equator on February 12–13, 1521. Shortage of food and water as well as disease killed many more of the sailors and only Magellan's unvarying courage and confidence prevented mutiny. On March 6, they again sighted land and the sailors could see the silhouettes of canoes near the shore. All the food had gone, several men had died of scurvy, others were too sick to stand. As they drew closer to the tree-lined shore the men wept unashamedly. Magellan led them in singing their praise to God for their safe deliverance.

The shore looked friendly, but the men rowing the dozens of outrigger canoes, which had by now surrounded Magellan's ships, had a menacing appearance. The rowers were powerfully built and naked, and showed no fear as they swarmed up the *Trinidad's* sides and on board. Although the islanders were more curious than hostile, some of the Spaniards lost their nerve at the sight of them. The crew opened fire with their crossbows, killing some of the islanders and scattering the rest. Those who retreated, however, made away with a *skiff* (a small light boat), which led Magellan to give the name Ladrones (thieves) to the two islands sighted that day. They were probably Guam and Rota, in the southern Mariana Islands.

Next day Magellan led a landing party to recover the skiff. His party bombarded a village, setting a number of huts on fire and killing seven islanders. The Spaniards' display of force was effective. The skiff was recovered and the islanders offered provisions— yams, coconuts, pigs, and chickens—as well as fresh water. On March 9, the small fleet set sail again to the southwest. On that day the Englishman, Master Andrew, died.

One week later the ships sighted the island of St. Lazarus, known to us as Samar in the Philippine Islands. To the south lay the Moluccas, well charted waters, and safety. Magellan and his men had been the first Europeans to cross the Pacific. Their brave voyage was to end in tragedy. Magellan received no tribute from the ruler of Mactan, after forming alliances with other local Philippine rulers. So he attacked Mactan and there, on April 27, with Pigafetta as eye-witness, Magellan was killed by the islanders.

After Magellan's death, the expedition all but came to grief. Of the five ships that had set out from Spain, only one returned. Two ships had already been lost. The *Trinidad* attempted to get back to America and was captured by the Portuguese. The *Concepción* was scuttled in the Philippines. Only the *Victoria*, now commanded by Sebastian del Cano, one of the San Julián mutineers, managed to struggle back to Spain after the first circumnavigation of the world. It had taken three years, and of the many who set out, only 17 Europeans returned to Spain with del Cano.

The Crucifix and the Sword

5

Magellan's actual discoveries in the Pacific were modest but his voyage was an epic. It was clear to the Spanish that Portugal's hold on the Moluccas was unbreakable, so Spain resolved to tighten her own grip on the Philippine Islands. Several expeditions set out in the wake of Magellan. The first, in 1525, was commanded by Garcia Jofre de Loyasa, with del Cano, a survivor of Magellan's voyage, as a member of the crew. But of the seven ships that left Spain, only four reached the Pacific, and only two crossed the ocean. Both de Loyasa and del Cano died before the flagship, *Santa Maria de la Victoria*, finally limped into the Spice Islands.

Hernando Cortes, the conqueror of Mexico, had long wanted to voyage to the East Indies. When he heard that Loyasa had entered the Pacific, he went ahead, and three ships sailed from Mexico on October 31, 1527. But it was another ill-fated enterprise. Two of the ships disappeared in a gale 3,000 miles from port. The third, the *Florida*, commanded by Alvaro de Saavedra, succeeded at least in reaching the Moluccas. Saavedra made contact with survivors of the Loyasa expedition and sailed on June 3, 1528, in an attempted

return voyage to North America. He ran into the teeth of the north-east trade winds and had to return to the Moluccas. The following summer Saavedra tried again, steering a more southerly course and skirting the north coast of New Guinea. The same coast had been sighted three years before by the Portuguese Jorge de Meneses, who was blown off course on his way to the Moluccas. Saavedra described the Papuans, the native inhabitants of New Guinea, as "cannibals with frizzled hair." The cannibals did, however, provide the expedition with food probably consisting of fresh fruit, vegetables, and fish, or meat from wild pigs. From Papua, Saavedra sailed on to the northeast, sighting a number of islands in the Admiralty and Marshall groups. The crew of the *Florida* landed on what may have been one of the Marshall Islands. There the islanders were light skinned, the men with painted arms and bodies, the women with long black hair. The strangers from the sea were welcomed with dancing and singing, and because Saavedra had fallen sick the crew stayed there for eight days. Attempts to go on farther east were thwarted by adverse winds which blew them back yet again to the

Following Magellan's voyage across the Pacific in 1520 – 1521, other Spanish expeditions set out to search for the much-sought-after Spice Islands and other islands in the vast Pacific Ocean. This contemporary illustration shows Hernando de Grijalva embarking from Mexico in 1537.

Papuans are a Melanesian people living in New Guinea. In their own language, their name means "frizzled," describing their hair. They are skilled boatbuilders and have constructed fine suspension bridges across rivers. The villages are kept clean and are decorated with shrubs. Some even have a small "village square," with stone seats for passing travelers.

Moluccas. This time the crew were without their captain, for Saavedra had died at sea.

Spain seemed doomed to such failures. Another expedition from Mexico under Hernando de Grijalva met a similar fate in 1537. The sailors sighted several small islands, probably in the Gilbert group, but Grijalva was murdered by his crew and his ship was wrecked off New Guinea. A five-ship expedition, commanded by Ruy Lopez de Villalobos, departed from Mexico in 1542 and reached the Spice Islands, but an attempted return journey failed. The chronicler of that voyage was an Italian named Juan Gaetano, later hailed by his countrymen as the discoverer of the Hawaiian Islands. There was never any conclusive proof of such an exploit, however, and Gaetano can hardly claim to be included in the list of Pacific discoverers.

Despite these disasters Spain was still determined to have a share

in the trade of the Orient. In 1564–1565, another expedition sailed from Mexico with the object of colonizing the Philippine Islands and establishing them once and for all within the Spanish sphere of influence. The expedition was also instructed to find the best return route. Miguel Lopez de Legaspi led the expedition, which included a number of friars prepared to convert heathen populations to Christianity, if need be with the support of the sword. In the 500-ton flagship *San Pedro* sailed Andres de Urdaneta, a survivor of the Loyasa expedition. He would have been commander of the voyage had he not been precluded by having taken holy orders. The smallest vessel, the 40-ton *San Lucas*, captained by a somewhat disreputable nobleman named Alonso de Arellano, became separated from the rest of the fleet only nine days after sailing. It was, however, to make its own contribution to the history of the Pacific.

The remaining ships proceeded smoothly on their course to the

Spain sent out experienced men in sturdy, well-equipped ships to search for new lands and profitable trade routes. But despite all their care, ships were blown off course and men died of scurvy and other diseases. This engraving shows the seven ships of the Loyasa expedition leaving for the Moluccas in 1525. None of his ships completed the voyage.

Philippines. Legaspi founded two Spanish colonies, the first in Cebu, the second in Manila. The initial landing was achieved without bloodshed, but later there were clashes with the islands' inhabitants. Such heathen uprisings were dealt with in the style we nowadays associate with the remorseless conquistadors. Nevertheless, on the whole, Legaspi's colonizing mission was a success. Despite protests by Portugal, the islands were finally recognized as belonging to Spain.

Legaspi, however, played no part in the events which proved to be as significant as the settlement itself. The little *San Lucas*, whether accidentally or deliberately lost, arrived in the Philippine Islands some weeks before Legaspi and his ships. According to the mutilated log book kept by the captain, Arellano, and his pilot, Lope Martin,

Above: this Spanish carrack was typical of the ships sent out on expeditions in the 1500's. Notice the pilot on the top deck taking a sight with his sextant.

Left: The Philippines are an island country where boats are a main form of transportation. The islands have many natural harbors, but some are made dangerous by the coral reefs across the mouth of the harbor.

the *San Lucas* set sail on a return voyage to North America on April 22, 1565. Taking advantage of the southwesterly summer winds, the ships reached the Mariana Islands and then headed north, skirting the coast of Japan and picking up the westerlies beyond latitude 40°. Thanks to these winds and the eastward-flowing Japan current, they made landfall in America on July 17. Then they sailed on to Acapulco, the main port on the Mexican coast.

Urdaneta, on board the *San Pedro*, now commanded by Felipe de Salcedo, followed a similar route and arrived back in America on October 3, reaching Mexico about three months later than Arellano. Both ships had accomplished the unprecedented feat of sailing across the Pacific from west to east. It suited historians to give Urdaneta sole credit for this enterprise. They said that Arellano had been lucky whereas Urdaneta had followed a plan. After receiving a hero's welcome, Arellano was charged with disobedience and defection.

The important fact established by both ships was that a practicable sea route for a west-east crossing of the Pacific did exist. The discovery was to lay the foundation for Spanish trade with the Far East. In future, the treasure galleons loaded with silver would sail from Mexico early in the year via Guam in the Mariana Islands, to the Philippine Islands, returning along the high latitudes during the midsummer monsoons. The long and difficult return voyage might take anything from four to seven months, and strong convoys were needed to protect the galleons from marauding buccaneers. But for

Above: a Chinese porcelain goddess. Porcelain from China was one of the luxury goods that Spanish galleons carried across the Pacific from the Philippine Islands to Mexico during the late 1500's.

Above: the ships of the type that Mendaña and Quiros used to cross the Pacific Ocean were tiny in comparison with a modern ship like the Queen Elizabeth II. The sailing ship rarely exceeded 300 tons and could carry less than 150 men. The QE II has a tonnage of 65,983 tons and carries a crew of about 1,000, as well as 1,840 passengers.

Left: a more detailed sketch of a ship similar to that used by Mendaña.

This map, drawn by Ortelius in 1570, shows the supposed continent *Terra Australis Incognita.* Tierra del Fuego was discovered by Magellan when he sailed through the strait, but the rest of the coastline shows what the cartographers felt should be there, and almost reaches the equator.

30 or 40 years the galleons carried their cargoes of silver to Manila in the Philippine Islands and returned to Mexico laden with spices from the Moluccas and precious silks, brocades, velvets, ivory, and porcelain from China. This tremendously profitable trade continued until Spanish sea power was challenged by Holland. When the Dutch began importing silk and other luxuries by the Indian Ocean and Cape route, Spain's Pacific commerce was dealt a death blow.

During the 1500's Spain was obsessed—just as Holland, France, and England were to be in their turn—by the lure of the unknown

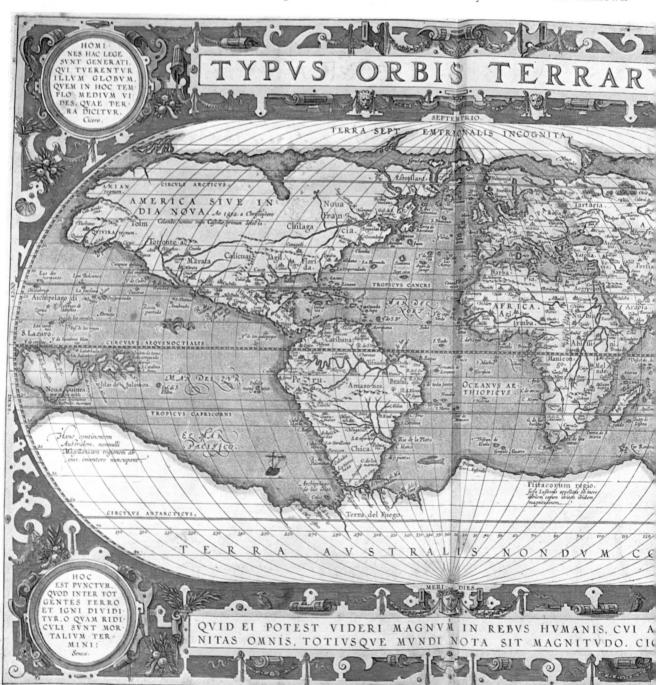

Right: according to local legend, the ancestors of this child reached the Ellice Islands (now Tuvalu) 27 generations ago.

Southern Continent. All contemporary mapmakers, including such men as Mercator and Ortelius, were confident that a great land mass must exist in the south. Their reasoning was that there had to be something to balance the continents of the Northern Hemisphere and keep the globe steady. They called it *Terra Australis Incognita*, the unknown southland. It was marked boldly, though fancifully, on their maps and charts. Through the years, legends multiplied concerning the fantastic vegetable and mineral wealth in store for the first nation to set foot on its shores.

Pedro Sarmiento de Gamboa, a historian, mathematician, and astronomer, persuaded the Spanish government to mount an expedition in 1567 with the express purpose of searching for *Terra Australis*. Sarmiento was deeply versed in Inca history and legend, and was convinced that such a gigantic continent stretched from some point west of Tierra del Fuego northwest to within 15° of the equator, and lay within easy sailing distance from Peru. Sarmiento, however, was impossibly self-centered and inflexible. Though he was a member of the expedition, he never forgave the authorities for passing him over as leader and selecting instead a man 11 years younger. This man was the 25-year-old Álvaro de Mendaña, relatively inexperienced but the nephew of the viceroy of Peru.

On November 19, 1567, Mendaña's two ships sailed from Callao in Peru. On board the 107-ton *Todos Santos* (all saints) and the 250-ton *Los Reyes* (the kings) were 150 men. Seventy were experienced sailors and soldiers and the remainder South American Indian slaves. Four Franciscan friars went with them to "convert all infidels." For three weeks the ships sailed steadily westward. Then, contrary to Sarmiento's counsel, but on the advice of Mendaña's pilot Hernán Gallego, an experienced navigator, they changed course to the northwest. Sarmiento later blamed the failure of the expedition on Mendaña and his officers for having ignored his advice at this point. Certainly, had they pressed on due west, they could hardly have avoided discovering the Society Islands, later found by Captain Wallis. As it was, the ships passed between the Marquesas and Tuamotu Islands, missing every island except a small atoll in the Ellice group (now Tuvalu) which they named Isle of Jesus. By now, after 57 days at sea, nerves were frayed. The drinking water was turning foul. An error on the part of Gallego, which prevented the crews landing on the Isle of Jesus, hardly improved matters.

This ornament from the Solomon Islands represented the protector spirit of the canoe and was attached to the prow above the water line. It is made of blackened wood inlaid with mother-of-pearl, and comes from Mararo Lagoon in New Georgia.

Near-wreckage on a line of coral reefs reinforced the crew's mutterings of complaint and mutiny. But happily, on the 80th day at sea, February 7, 1568, Gallego himself sighted land. A signal was hoisted to inform the *Los Reyes* and both crews joined in singing the *Te Deum*—a hymn of praise and thanksgiving to God.

As the ships entered a broad, palm-fringed bay, Mendaña was certain they had reached the shores of the elusive continent itself. It was only after a few days, when the interior had been explored, that it became evident that they had landed on an island. They named it Santa Isabel in honor of their patron saint. On arrival the ships were met by a fleet of canoes, full of frizzy-haired islanders armed with bows and arrows. The islanders swarmed aboard, clambered up the rigging, and eagerly exchanged gifts and greetings. Next day the local chief, Bilebanara, made an appearance, promising fresh provisions and water. When two days later the expected supplies had still not arrived Mendaña sent his camp master, Pedro de Ortega, ashore with an armed party. Although the landing party was hospitably received, no provisions were forthcoming.

Gallego meanwhile had begun the building of a five-ton brigantine, the *Santiago*, designed to undertake survey work closer to the shore. Sarmiento and Ortega embarked on less peaceful missions. The scouting parties they led failed to achieve any understanding with the local population. On one occasion the Spaniards were so sickened by a gift of a child's shoulder and arm—evidently proffered in good faith—that they wanted to put such heathens to the sword. This attitude angered Mendaña, who was more humane than Sarmiento.

Ortega and Gallego now took the *Santiago* on three exploratory cruises, during which many more islands were discovered. Among them were Malaita, Guadalcanal (named by Ortega after his birthplace in Spain), and St. George's Island. After a month it was decided to move camp to Guadalcanal. Once again the familiar pattern of events asserted itself—friendly approaches, misunderstandings, ambushes, kidnapings, and retaliations. Islanders were killed, huts and canoes were burned, and no colony was established. The ships moved on to San Cristóbal, and the same things happened. In the end, Mendaña, fatally irresolute, summoned a meeting to debate the next step. He himself was prepared to continue south in search of Sarmiento's southern continent. Sarmiento, supported by some of

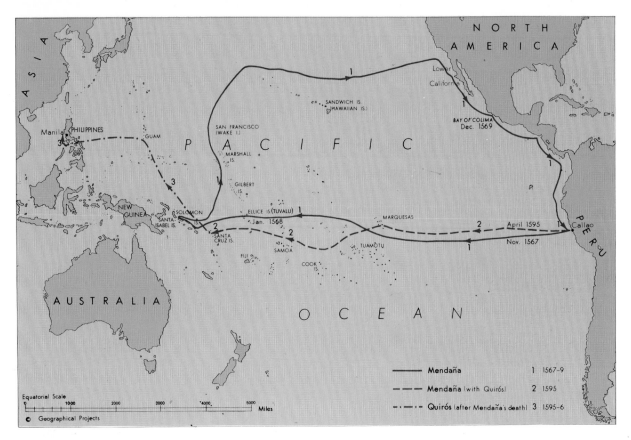

The voyages of Mendaña and Quiros in the Pacific Ocean in the 1500's.

the soldiers, preferred to stay, hoping to discover gold. Gallego, Ortega, and the friars advised turning back. In Gallego's estimation neither ship was sound enough to venture farther afield. Mendaña accepted this advice. A few islanders were captured as trophies of the voyage, the brigantine was burned, and at dawn on August 11 they sailed for Peru. After their departure, these islands remained unvisited by Europeans for another 200 years.

But the last stage of the voyage was by far the worst. The pilots were soon at loggerheads over the proper course to steer. Sarmiento suggested sailing southwest and was again overruled. Gallego defiantly refused to obey Mendaña's orders to set a course southeast, insisting that the only chance of safety lay in making for North America or Mexico by the northern route. For a time an unhappy compromise was followed as the ships veered to and fro between north and southeast, according to the wind. Finally Gallego's advice was heeded. The ships turned north, across the equator, past the Marshall and Gilbert groups and a lonely island which they named San Francisco (now Wake Island). Finally, they turned east in the zone of the seasonal westerlies. At some stage Sarmiento, perhaps deliberately, parted company with his chief. Mendaña and Gallego were left in the *Los Reyes* to battle through an appalling hurricane and then to cope with rapidly dwindling supplies of food and water as well as scurvy. Only Mendaña's encouraging promises of land near at hand staved off mutiny. At last came a sign that there was land nearby—they saw a clean pine log bobbing in the waves. Thirst-quenching rain followed shortly afterwards. On December 19, after four months at sea, the *Los Reyes* sighted the coast of Lower California. As the *Los Reyes* lay at anchor in the bay of Santiago de Colima, the *Todos Santos* limped in, almost a derelict.

It was nine months before the ships returned to Callao. Before reaching there, on Mendaña's orders, Sarmiento was arrested. He was later released and continued a violent and unsuccessful career at sea against the English. Mendaña himself received scant recognition for his eventful voyage "for," wrote a Spanish official to the king, "in my opinion . . . the islands they discovered were of little importance, although they say they heard of better lands; for in the course of these discoveries they found no specimens of spices, nor of gold and silver, nor of merchandise, nor of any other source of profit, and all the people were naked savages." The same writer, nevertheless, not Mendaña, first invented the name of the Solomon Islands for the newly discovered group. We can only guess his reason. Perhaps it was a fanciful association with the biblical King Solomon's fabled land of Ophir, reputed source of inexhaustible riches.

In any case Mendaña was not to be so easily fobbed off. In 1569, he returned with his uncle to Spain to plead at the royal court for another expedition. It took five years for him to obtain the royal assent to a new colonizing venture and another three for him to get back to Panama with his ships and volunteers. Then disaster struck. As he prepared to embark for Peru he was arrested and flung into prison on some trifling charge. When he was set free a new Peruvian viceroy demolished his plans. It was to be another 18 years before Mendaña sailed again. By then, Spanish claims to monopolize the eastern Pacific had received a rude shock. England, in the person of the irrepressible buccaneer Sir Francis Drake, had made a dramatic entry onto the scene.

English writers and mariners were also excited by the bait of *Terra Australis*. But the quest for a Northwest Passage into the Pacific was even more challenging. During Henry VIII's reign

Left: boatbuilders were important men in any port. But in Mexico they were doubly so. After long voyages, Spanish ships often limped into Spain's Mexican ports in desperate need of repair. It was the job of these boatbuilders to make the ships seaworthy again quickly.

(1509–1547), Robert Thorne and Roger Barlow had proposed a voyage to the Indies by this route and down through the Strait of Anian, popularly supposed to divide America and Asia. Now a new scheme was put forward to Queen Elizabeth I whereby England might annex *Terra Australis* by sailing through the Strait of Magellan. There, the plan was to trade and plunder as opportunity offered, and return through the Strait of Anian. After delaying for three years, Elizabeth finally entrusted Drake with the command of such an expedition. She instructed him to explore any lands not owned by Spain and to return via either America or the Moluccas. Drake interpreted his orders more flexibly than the queen had perhaps intended, and turned a voyage of discovery into a glorious privateering adventure.

On December 13, 1577, Drake sailed off in his 100-ton *Pelican*,

Decisions concerning New World expeditions and voyages were made at the Spanish court. The pattern of life was entirely different from that on board ship or in the colonies. It is little wonder that noblemen found it difficult to understand the reasons for the failures of ships and explorers.

Sir Francis Drake (1540?–1596) was the first Englishman to sail round the world. It was thought at first that the voyage was for the sole purpose of plundering Spanish ports. But documents indicate that he had received orders from his queen, Elizabeth I, to promote English trade in the Pacific and possibly claim new territories for England.

with four other ships—the *Elizabeth*, 80 tons, the *Swan*, 50 tons, the *Marygold*, 30 tons, and a 15-ton pinnace. They captured a Portuguese vessel near the Cape Verde Islands off Africa, and then cruised down the east coast of South America. Magellan had faced a mutiny in the port of San Julián. Drake faced a similar situation in the same place. The mutiny was crushed, but two store ships were broken up. When the remaining vessels emerged from the Strait of Magellan into a far from placid Pacific, gales drove them southeastward. The *Marygold* was sunk, the *Elizabeth* had drifted off course, and Drake was left alone in his flagship *Pelican*, now renamed the *Golden Hind*. There was no sight of land farther south. Drake was convinced he had reached the extremity of the American continent, and the meeting place of two oceans. It is doubtful whether Drake ever sighted Cape Horn, but he guessed rightly that Tierra del Fuego was an island and not part of a southern continent. The latter remained as elusive as ever. Drake spent several profitable months raiding the west coast from Chile to Mexico, plundering ships and towns. Then, laden with more wealth than any privateer had ever carried, he turned north to look for the northwest passage. Gales drove him to North America around 48°N. He then sailed to the San Francisco area and annexed it as New Albion. On July 23, 1579, after a five-week refitting period, Drake set a course southwest and then west to the Philippine Islands and the Moluccas. At Ternate in the North Moluccas he took on six tons of cloves, and, after nearly being shipwrecked on a reef, returned to England on September 26, 1580, back to glory and a knighthood. The political repercussions of his findings were considerable.

Drake's circumnavigation of the world was duplicated in 1586–1588 by Thomas Cavendish in the *Desire*, touching at the Philippine and Ladrone Islands, the Moluccas, and Java. A second voyage with John Davis was a failure, as was Sir Richard Hawkins' venture in 1593–1594. The English retired from the Pacific for 100 years.

The remarkably patient Mendaña made his second appearance at the end of the 1500's. Now 53 years old, holding the title of governor, he sailed from Callao on April 9, 1595, to colonize the "Isles of Solomon" he had discovered a quarter of a century previously. He was given two large ships, the flagship *San Jeronimo* and the *San Ysabel*, the smaller frigate *Santa Catalina*, and the galiot *San Felipe*, a vessel which could be propelled by sails and by oars. In all there

The plaque with which Drake claimed the coast of present-day California for England in 1579, naming it New Albion. He was greeted by a tribe of Indians who exchanged presents with the sailors. The Indians became so friendly in the time it took to repair Drake's ships that they were reluctant to see the white men go.

were 378 people under his command. They included sailors, soldiers, private citizens willing to fight for money, and priests, as well as a motley collection of potential settlers. Some were respectable married couples, others unemployed adventurers, and some prostitutes. Mendaña's wife, Doña Ysabel Barreto, a bad-tempered, high-strung woman, insisted on accompanying her husband. He was also saddled with three brothers-in-law, one of whom, Don Lorenzo Barreto, captained the flagship. The camp master was an elderly soldier, a courageous but highly impetuous and quarrelsome man. Only in his choice of pilot was Mendaña fortunate. He was a 30-year-old Portuguese, born in the slums of Lisbon, Pedro Fernandez de Quiros by name.

Mendaña guaranteed that the islands he was looking for were not more than 1,450 leagues (about 4,350 nautical miles) west of Peru. Yet, when on July 21, having traveled little more than half this distance, the expedition reached a group of beautiful islands, he seriously believed he had rediscovered the Solomon Islands. When he realized his mistake he named them Las Marquesas de Mendoza (now shortened to the Marquesas) after the viceroy of Peru who had backed his venture. The islanders were light skinned, long-haired, and muscular, naked, and tattooed with blue dye. Both Mendaña and Quiros were charmed by their manners, and impressed by their well-constructed canoes. But the camp master and his men

ARCTIC CIRCLE

BERING SEA

A S I A

JAPAN

PACIFIC

TROPIC OF CANCER

5c

5c

3a

3a

4

SAN FRANCISCO BAY

5c

40°

4

8a

LUZON

Manila

PHILIPPINES

5a

8a

5d

SAMAR

5a

1A

8a 2

MINDANAO

BORNEO

EQUATOR

8a

Ternate

HALMAHERA

7a

0°

LADRONES
(MARIANAS)

8a

4 2

SAN FRANCISCO
(WAKE I.)

1

8a

4

SANDWICH IS.
(HAWAIIAN IS.)

CAROLINE IS.

5a

MARSHALL
ISLANDS

3a

2?

5c

2

1

LINE ISLANDS

OCEAN

2

8b

ADMIRALTY
IS.

GILBERT
ISLANDS

NEW
GUINEA

8b

6

NEW IRELAND

7a

6

NEW
BRITAIN

SANTA
ISABEL IS.

SOLOMON
ISLANDS

PHOENIX
IS.

6

JAVA

6

7a

1A

7b

TIMOR

7b

8b

LOUISIADE
ARCHO.

5d

SANTA
CRUZ IS.

5a

3a

ELLICE (TUVALU)
ISLANDS

3a

MARQUESAS

3b

8a

8a

GULF
OF
CARPEN-
TARIA

5c

5b

NEW
HEBRIDES

6

7a

HORN
IS.

SAMOA

3b

5b

3b

TUAMOTU

3a

1A 8b

Dampier
Land

ESPIRITU SANTO

5d

FIJI

FRIENDLY IS.
(TONGA)

6

COOK
ISLANDS

SOCIETY
ISLANDS

TAHITI

PUKAPUKA

1

6

NEW

7b

TROPIC OF CAPRICORN

NEW
CALEDONIA

TUBUAI
IS.
(AUSTRAL IS.)

PITCAIRN I.

5b

HOLLAND

AUSTRALIA

TASMAN

INDIAN

7a

40°

OCEAN

VAN DIEMEN'S LAND
(TASMANIA)

7a

SEA

NEW
ZEALAND

7a

140°

180°

140°

		Magellan			1	1519–21

Del Cano (after Magellan's death)   1A 1521–2

Saavedra   2 1527–9

Mendaña   3a 1567–9
Mendaña (with Quirós)   3b 1595

Drake   4 1577–80

Quirós (after Mendaña's death)   5a 1595–6

Quirós (with Torres)   5b 1605–6
Quirós (after leaving Torres)   5c 1606
Torres (after departure of Quirós)   5d 1606

Schouten & Le Maire   6 1615–7

Tasman (with Visscher)   7a 1642–3
Tasman (with Visscher)   7b 1644

Dampier   8a 1686–91
Dampier   8b 1699–1700

Left: the Pacific Ocean, showing the voyages of European explorers, from Magellan in the early 1500's to the Englishman William Dampier in 1700.

Caca Fogo.

Caca Plata.

Above: on his round-the-world voyage Drake spent several months plundering the coast of South America. Here, his flagship the *Golden Hind* is seen capturing a Spanish treasure ship.

could not resist an occasional demonstration of force. There were frequent clashes, and Quiros was deeply disgusted by a soldier who was about to fire on an islander simply because he enjoyed killing. During the Spaniards' two-week stay in the islands, the Marquesans had cause to regret their first encounter with white men. Quiros admitted that some 200 islanders had been killed.

The ships sailed on, sighting only uninhabited atolls in the Ellice group. The crews became surly and restless, the sailors at odds with the soldiers. Quiros was criticized for general incompetence, Mendaña for baseless optimism. On September 7, the ships ran into dense fog. When it cleared, the *Santa Ysabel* had vanished without trace. That same evening the *San Jeronimo* sighted a tree-covered island. Beyond it was a smoking volcano which erupted a few days later. Mendaña's renewed hope that the island which erupted might be part of the Solomon Islands was reinforced by the appearance of islanders in outrigger canoes. They were much darker than the Marquesans encountered earlier, with frizzy hair and red-dyed

Above: the vast Pacific Ocean is the home of about 80 per cent of the world's active volcanoes. It is small wonder that many of the volcanic islands are uninhabited. In 1883 Krakatoa, west of Java, erupted, killing 36,000 people. Walls were cracked in Batavia 100 miles away, and shock waves traveled three times round the world before dissipating.

Left: the Marquesas are a series of volcanic islands. The inhabitants are handsome, light-skinned Polynesians, who welcomed the early visitors from the other side of the world.

teeth. But Mendaña was wrong again. The islands now reached formed a new and separate group, lying north of the New Hebrides. The largest of them, which Mendaña named Santa Cruz, is known today as Ndeni.

The very first encounter with the islanders caused bloodshed when they shot arrows into the rigging of the ship. The soldiers retaliated with fire from handguns, called *arquebuses*.

When the Spanish anchored in Graciosa Bay, however, the islanders appeared to be friendly. The chieftain Malope was paddled out and gifts were exchanged. At night the Spaniards watched their fires and listened to them singing and dancing. But once more there was no mutual understanding or trust. A watering party was ambushed and three men wounded. Mendaña promptly dispatched a punishment party to burn huts, kill islanders, and steal pigs. The rest of the men tried to hack down some trees and set up a camp, but the atmosphere was tense with anxiety and bad feeling. The camp master was a law to himself, Mendaña was sick with malaria, his deputy Quiros was continually harassed. The men hankered for action and clamored to be taken to a Christian land, back to Peru or on to Manila.

Mendaña was fast losing his control of the situation, weakened by

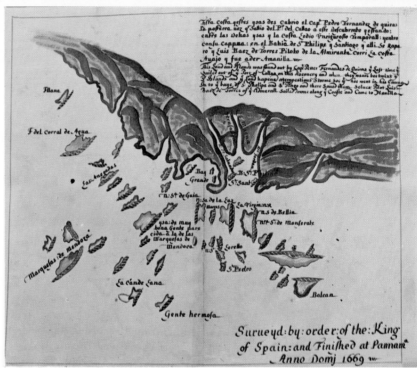

Right: during their voyage to Santa Cruz (Ndeni), Mendaña and Quiros found many small islands. The map was drawn in 1669 by William Hack. An Englishman, Hack drew his maps from Spanish information. Another example of Hack's work is the map of Acapulco, Mexico, opposite.

Below: Manila, present capital of the Philippines, was founded by Legaspi in 1571. It stands on one of the world's largest landlocked harbors and became an important port for expeditions.

disease and the constant nagging of his wife and her relatives. It was on their suggestion that he agreed to the fatal stabbing of the troublesome camp master. The death led to an orgy of killing, as supporters of both factions fell on one another. The climax was the return of a raiding party with the report that they had killed the chieftain Malope.

Quiros watched and recorded these horrors with growing alarm and despair. Malaria began to kill off many of the Spaniards, and on October 18, 1595, Mendaña himself died. He was buried with due honors, and his coffin was later taken to Manila. Quiros wrote his obituary, a curiously muted eulogy for a man whose actions tragically failed to measure up to his ideals. "He was a person," said Quiros, "zealous for the honor of God and the service of the King, to whom all things ill done did not appear well, nor did those well done appear evil. He was very plain spoken, not diffuse in giving his reasons . . . he did not want arguments but deeds."

Mendaña had handed over responsibility to his wife and her brother Don Lorenzo, but when he died some days later Quiros took charge. On November 18, with disease still raging, he and the remaining men sailed away from their "corner of hell" and made for the Philippine Islands. The wooden ships were rotting. Supplies were almost exhausted. Corpses were tossed overboard daily. Quiros was forced to consult Doña Ysabel on all matters. She refused to permit him to jettison the other ships and combine the crews. She would not allow the little fresh water they had to be distributed to the dying men, women, and children, but used it instead to wash her own clothes. By December the ships were near the equator. The days were stifling, the nights freezing. Rations were down to half a pound of flour and half a pint of putrid water a day. The *Santa Catalina* disappeared and was never traced. The *San Felipe* vanished for a time but later reached the Philippine Islands. Quiros, by a remarkable feat of navigation, brought the flagship to port. On New Year's Day, 1596, they arrived off the coast of Guam, but the ship's tackle was in such poor shape that they were unable to lower the boats. After renewed threats of mutiny, Doña Ysabel herself seemed resigned to death, spending the days at her devotions. Quiros begged her to hand over the only remaining fresh meat on board, a calf and two pet pigs. She yielded up the calf but refused to part with the pigs.

At last Manila was sighted. A boat carrying four Spaniards rowed out to meet them. To Quiros they were as welcome as "four thousand angels." The "angels" even managed to persuade Doña Ysabel to give up her pigs. Mendaña was reburied and his widow remarried very soon after. Then, after a return voyage of "incredible hardships and troubles," Quiros brought the *San Jeronimo* back to Acapulco on December 11, 1596. The fantastic voyage was over. It had been a sorry, blood-strewn failure. Quiros alone had salvaged from it some shreds of honor.

Acapulco was founded by the Spanish in 1550. It quickly became an important port for the Spanish fleets and the starting point for expeditions into the Pacific. This map of the settlement was drawn in the 1600's.

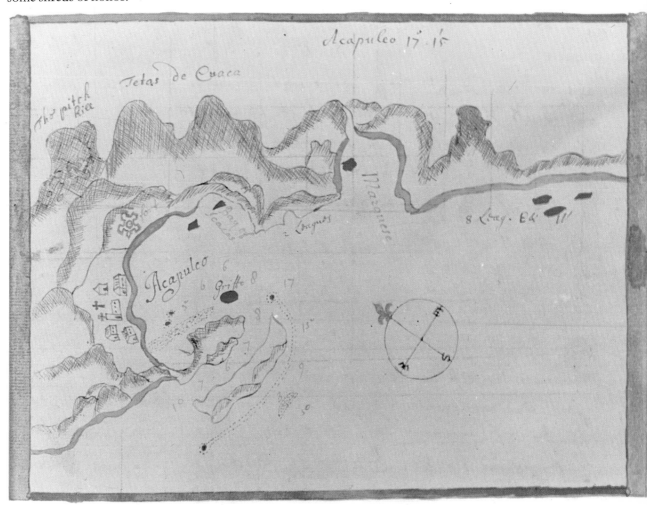

Spain's New Jerusalem

6

Quiros' unhappy experiences with Mendaña only fired his determination to return to the Pacific at the first opportunity. Unable to persuade either the viceroy of Peru or the king of Spain to finance him, he journeyed to Rome in 1600 as a simple pilgrim. He was interrogated there by a board of mathematicians, astronomers, and navigators who were sufficiently impressed by his knowledge to secure him an audience with the pope. The audience was successful. Armed with letters of recommendation and a piece of wood, believed to be from the cross on which Christ died, Quiros returned to the Spanish court. He was increasingly bent on finding the Southern Continent and converting its inhabitants to Christianity. And he was by now inspired with a fiery missionary zeal. Eventually his persistence won the day, although it was not until 1605 that he was given a command. He had three ships, the *San Pedro y Paulo*,

the *San Pedrico*, and a small pinnace about the size of a modern launch called *Los Tres Reyes*. The captain of the *San Pedrico* was a Spanish navigator named Luis Vaez de Torres. In command of the *Los Tres Reyes* was a former pilot, Bernal Cermeno. The chief pilot was Juan Ochoa de Bilboa, who, Quiros said, was "thrust on me against my will." There was also Quiros' loyal young poet-secretary, Luis de Belmonte Bermudez.

Quiros displayed a passion for the moral well-being of his men right from the start. The pattern of the expedition was set on December 21, 1605, the day of departure from Callao. The 300 soldiers and sailors were accompanied by six Franciscans and four friars of the Order of St. John to tend the sick. There were no women on board. Quiros insisted that all officers don friars' habit at the quayside. Banners were unfurled and all on the ships and the shore

The city of Rome in the 1600's. It was to Rome that Quiros traveled in 1600, having unsuccessfully approached the viceroy of Peru and the king of Spain, to persuade the Pope to support his next expedition to the Pacific.

fell to their knees in prayer. A volley of musketry and cannon rang out, the crowds lining the beaches cheered, and the little fleet sailed proudly off westward.

Quiros' plan was to zig-zag in a generally southwesterly direction, altering course to northwest if no land was sighted. After reaching latitude 10°, he would again set course southwest and then northwest. If still no land appeared, they would then make for the Santa Cruz Islands. Quiros was a good navigator, but he was so preoccupied with applying his moral principles that he paid insufficient attention to the sailing of his ships. He forbade card playing or gambling in any form and ordered the backgammon boards to be thrown into the sea. He prohibited swearing and blaspheming and made attendance at the daily religious service compulsory. Such moralizing and spiritual chastizing did not endear Quiros either to his officers or to his men, with their rough, volatile temperaments and their single-minded interest in treasure and personal riches. Quiros was ready to apply the same ethical standards to their treatment of any islander encountered in the course of their voyage, directing his crew to "treat them as fathers do children." But ingrained prejudice against all heathens seemed only too likely to foil such praiseworthy intentions.

The sea remained calm until January 22, when they had reached latitude 26° south. Then the weather began to deteriorate. Under strong pressure from his dejected crew, but against the advice of Torres, Quiros changed course to west-northwest. This was probably the decision which lost the expedition the opportunity of important discoveries. There was the usual shortage of water, but this was alleviated for the first time on a sea voyage by using a distilling machine to give drinkable water. The only islands seen were uninhabited atolls in the Tuamotu Islands. They included those known today as Ducie, Henderson, Marutea, and Hao. On February 10, Quiros landed on Hao and goods were exchanged with the inhabitants. Eleven days later another island was explored which yielded plenty of fish and coconuts, but no fresh water. Mendaña had called it Island of Fish, but it was renamed later Caroline Island.

The dissatisfied sailors, urged on by the chief pilot, were on the verge of mutiny. Then, on the night of March 1, pinpoints of light from island fires were seen. Next morning land loomed up, a low island, obviously inhabited. The islanders paddled out in their canoes, singing as they came. But when they tried to take away the pinnace they had to be dispersed with musket fire. A subsequent landing also led to a clash. The Spaniards killed some islanders and a boat containing jugs of precious water capsized. Clearly a lengthy stay was inadvisable. Quiros named the island Gente Hermosa, after its handsome inhabitants. It is known today as Rakahanga, in the northern Cook group.

Although the weather improved, hunger and thirst were still serious problems. Quiros, now a sick man, refused to permit any "irreligious" diversions such as cards or dice. The chief pilot grew

Above: the playing cards that Quiros refused to permit would have looked much like these. Spanish playing cards in the 1600's were illustrated with *copas* (cups), *espadas* (swords), *oros* (money), and *bastos* (clubs). A pack consisted of 48 cards instead of 52.

Right: as European explorers anchored off a Pacific Island hundreds of islanders in their canoes would paddle out to meet them. The welcome the visitors received was not always friendly. The islanders used two types of canoes in their efforts to get as many men as possible out to the strange ships. The single canoe was often little more than a dugout tree trunk. The double canoes were two single canoes joined by a wooden platform and were propelled by both paddles and sails.

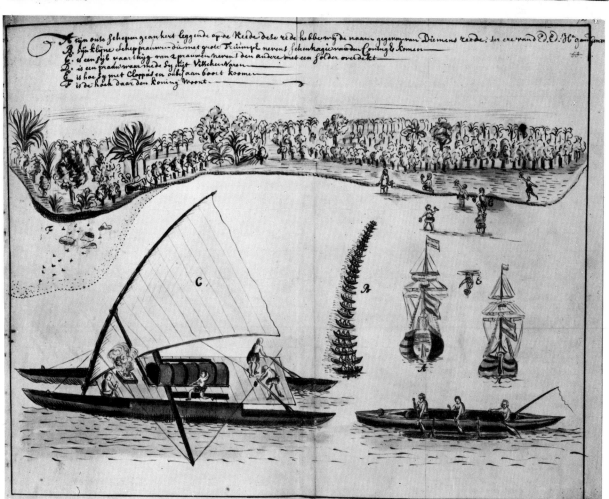

Above: when Quiros landed in Espiritu Santo in the New Hebrides, where the islanders live in mud huts, he thought he had found *Terra Australis*.
Below: this native bark painting comes from Banks Island in the New Hebrides.

so truculent that he had to be disarmed and sent on board the *San Pedrico* in irons. For three weeks there was no sight of land. Then, unexpectedly, it rained and, even more welcome, land appeared on the horizon. On April 7, the ships anchored in a pleasant bay. The islanders proved friendly, and their chief, Tumai, showed surprising familiarity with the Spanish firearms. Tumai provided Quiros with accurate sailing instructions. He spoke also of a large land to the south, which Quiros of course assumed to be the longed-for *Terra Australis*. After 10 days on the island, to which they gave the name of Nuestra Señora del Socorro—now Taumako in the Duff group—they sailed, restocked with water and provisions.

On May 1, the ships entered a wide bay. They anchored there two days later after a reconnoiter by Torres, who described the bay as "big enough for all the fleets in the world." Quiros named it the Bay of St. Philip and St. James. There was land on every side, with trees and mountains fading into the distance. Landing parties confirmed that it was a most beautiful place, with a broad river flowing into the bay, rolling plains and forests, and an abundance of plants and domestic animals. True, the islanders appeared none too friendly and some had to be killed. Quiros was undeterred, convinced that he had at last reached the land of his heart's desire. It had been granted to him to take possession of a great continent and to save its inhabitants from the damnation that awaited all heathen peoples.

In a strange ceremony, Quiros now made his men members of a new Holy Order of his own invention, the Knights of the Holy Ghost, who were to be dedicated to the ideals of chivalry. The crews complied, with what hidden feelings one can only imagine. After a night of dancing and celebration on board, with bells ringing, drums rolling, and fireworks exploding, Torres led a party ashore on the morning of Whit Sunday, May 14. Quiros followed with his officers and men. Amid the fluttering of the royal standard and massed banners, Quiros knelt and kissed the ground. "O Land," he cried, "sought for so long, intended to be found by many, and so desired by me!" Taking possession of the territory in the name of God, the Holy Orders, and King Philip III of Spain, who was also Archduke of Austria, Quiros named it Austrialia del Espiritu Santo. The colony he was about to establish would be called New Jerusalem and the nearby river the Jordan. Mass was celebrated, blessings were given, guns fired, and the ceremony was over. It was the climax of Quiros' life.

But disillusion was soon to set in. Don Diego de Prado y Tovar, an officer on the *San Pedrico*, never concealed his contempt for the whole proceeding, ridiculing Quiros and asserting that all they had found were black devils with poisoned arrows. Bilboa, the pilot, was still under arrest but ever a source of danger. The surroundings were undeniably beautiful, but there were no signs of the promised riches. The

The natives of the New Hebrides are Melanesian. They live in small tribes and each tribe refuses to recognize the authority of the others. At the beginning of this century cannibalism still existed on the islands of Espiritu Santo, Malekula, and Pentecost Island.

Sharks were unknown to European explorers until they reached the warm waters of the Pacific and South Atlantic. The largest fish in the sea, sharks have an almost continuous hunger. Early explorers found that many sharks are man-eaters.

feast of Corpus Christi was celebrated and Belmonte Bermudez penned a graceful poem as Quiros continued to sing the praises of his "healthy and fertile land." Quiros did not yet realize, though some of his men suspected it, that his "continent" was yet another Pacific island—to be accurate, two islands. Espiritu Santo, Santo for short, was the largest island in a group that was later to be called the New Hebrides. To the south—seemingly part of the same land mass—lay the second largest island, Malekula.

After the feast there followed a series of events for which there has never been a satisfactory explanation. True, Quiros was sick and so were many of his crew. True, also, efforts to placate the islanders had been unavailing. Mutiny was ever a possibility. The situation was undeniably bad. But what Quiros appeared to do was to abandon all he had labored so hard to create. Early in June, three weeks after landing, all three ships set sail again, ostensibly to discover more lands to windward. With Quiros went two island boys. When one of them pleaded to be returned to his family, he was sternly lectured by Quiros: "Silence, child! You know not what you ask. Greater good awaits you than the sight of heathen parents and friends and their communion!" Whatever this "good" was the boys were never to discover since they died shortly after the expedition's arrival home.

Quiros may have intended to return to New Jerusalem for the winter. Later he said that a sudden worsening of the weather prevented him putting back to shore. During the night of June 11, the lights of the anchored *San Pedrico* and the *Los Tres Reyes* vanished. By the morning the *San Pedro y Paulo* was alone at sea, out of sight of land. Don Diego later hinted at a mutiny but there is not a scrap of evidence to support this. More probably there was negligence on the pilot's part. Quiros apparently wished to continue westward but was overruled. He missed the Santa Cruz Islands, and turned north to latitude 38°, and then continued east by the normal galleon route to Acapulco, which he eventually reached on November 23, 1606.

Far from being hailed as a hero, Quiros was assailed by critics and enemies, and left to wander through Mexico. He eventually arrived back in Spain, penniless. Of his strength of purpose there had never been any doubt. Of his fitness to lead men and to take positive decisions there is much question. Yet he certainly did not deserve the abuse heaped on him by rivals such as the arrogant Don Diego, who branded him as an upstart Portuguese lunatic, a liar, fraud, and traitor. Quiros battled on for recognition of his achievements,

When the Spanish landed in Mexico the Indians soon became unpaid servants to the strange white men from across the sea. This illustration, from a Spanish manuscript, shows the Indians' view of their new masters. The Indians are working steadily while their Spanish overseers stand over them with long, wagging tongues.

convinced that his "continent" should be settled and exploited. He was given vague promises, and shuttled to and fro between the Council of State and the Council of the Indies. Finally, in October 1614, he was granted permission to return home to Peru. By now he was too old and sick anyway. On the voyage to Panama he died, his head still full of an imaginary empire in the Pacific big enough to hold 30 million people and ripe with untold riches. But his superiors knew only too well that the Spanish treasury was almost exhausted.

Yet there was an important epilogue to Quiros' voyage. On the morning of June 12, 1606, Don Diego and Torres had awakened to find Quiros gone. A search for possible wreckage was made far enough along the coast to convince them that Espiritu Santo was merely an island. Two weeks later they opened sealed instructions from the viceroy, directing them to continue looking for land southward as far as latitude 20° south. If they were unsuccessful they were to return to Spain via the Philippine and Spice Islands. Torres, a more decisive and resolute man than Quiros, took charge of the operation. The voyagers sailed down to latitude 21° south in bitterly cold weather, and were then forced back to the northwest. Torres now planned to sail along the north coast of New Guinea, a land that had been already claimed for Spain in 1545 by Inigo Ortiz de Retes. But strong headwinds prevented their rounding the eastern tip of New Guinea and they changed course. Torres observed: "I could not weather the east point, so I coasted along to the westward on the south side." This simple statement concealed a sensational discovery. For as they battled in intense heat through seas infested by sharks and littered with dangerous reefs, Torres unwittingly hit upon the southern coast of New Guinea and proved it to be an enormous island and not part of a great continent. From mid-July till the end of September they charted a coast never seen by Europeans and claimed it for the Spanish crown. The naked islanders were in the main wild and unfriendly, but as the voyagers approached the western tip of the island Torres reported the islanders to be "more civilized," with better ornaments, some of Chinese origin. Some of the islanders Torres described as "Mahometans" who conceived it their duty to conquer and convert the heathens known as "Papuans." Torres assumed correctly that they were now near the Moluccas. They sailed on to Banda, then to Ternate, and reached Manila on May 22, 1607.

It was the Scottish geographer Alexander Dalrymple who, over a century later, first gave the name of Torres Strait to the passage through which the *San Pedrico* had sailed. The exact route was never ascertained. The significance of the discovery was not recognized. And not until the time of Captain Cook did any nation, apart from Spain, learn of Torres' voyage. Of Torres himself, nothing further is known. Even in Spain, perhaps only Quiros was excited by the news of his former captain's exploit. But eight years later Quiros was dead, and the great age of Spanish discovery and conquest was buried with him.

Right: this 1589 map shows the Solomon Islands, New Guinea, and a mysterious passage in exactly the position of the strait Torres discovered 17 years later. The passage is shown as a straight, clear channel between New Guinea and Australia. The real Torres Strait is reef-strewn and presents such a navigational challenge that even today it is not routinely used.

Above: the magnificent Spanish
Armada that sailed toward England in
1588 was defeated by a combination of
English skill and catastrophic weather.
The defeat brought to an end Spanish
supremacy at sea.

Right: this engraving from the 1600's
shows Dutch cartographers at work.

The Dutch in the Pacific

7

In the year 1581, The Netherlands, under the leadership of the House of Orange, declared itself independent of Spain. Seven years later the Spanish Armada, sent out to ferry an invasion army across the English Channel, was routed by the English fleet. Spain's great days of foreign adventure were over. Henceforth the mastery of the seas was to be disputed· between the English and Dutch navies. During the 1600's, although the English staked their claim in the Indian Ocean, it was the Dutch who were to monopolize the East Indies trade and so to dominate the Pacific.

The Dutch merchants and seamen who ousted the Portuguese from their Far East strongholds were of a far different caliber from the Spanish conquistadors. Not for them the sword and the Bible. If the Dutch carried anything, it was a pair of scales and a ledger. For the Dutch were businessmen and what they sought were new markets and trade routes. They had already had an important share in the carrying trade from the East. But their regular sea routes were abruptly closed when Philip II united the crowns of Spain and Portugal in 1580. Newly-won political freedom as well as economic necessity now led the Dutch to challenge Portugal's waning power in the Orient. They were by tradition hardy seamen and they were far more advanced in the fields of shipbuilding and cartography than either Spain or Portugal. Cornelius Houtman's expedition of 1595 successfully ran the gauntlet of Portuguese naval strength off the Cape of Good Hope. Similar trading ventures underlined Dutch determination to seek their destiny in the East.

In 1602, the powerful Dutch East India Company was formed to coordinate policy. The Company was granted virtually sovereign powers. It was given exclusive rights to trade in the Indies. Sanction

Above: a Dutch trader and his wife, accompanied by their Javanese servant, survey the ships of the Dutch East India Company in the port of Batavia. From the time it was incorporated, the company was a great commercial success.

This battered pewter plaque was found over a hundred years after Dirk Hartog left it on the island named for him. It records the visits of two Dutch ships to the desolate island.

was granted it to wage war against Spain and Portugal and to maintain its own armed forces on land and sea. It was able to establish trading posts and colonies, to make treaties, to coin money, and to wield administrative, judicial, and legal authority over the areas it controlled. The Company flourished for almost two centuries before being taken over by the Dutch government in 1798, but its greatest achievements were seen in the 1600's. The Portuguese were driven from Ceylon and the Spice Islands. The Company set up factories or trading posts in the Persian Gulf, in India, in the Malayan Archipelago, and in Formosa. In 1619, one governor general of the Dutch East Indies, Jan Coen, founded the city of Batavia, on the site of the old town of Jacatra, on the island of Java. And Batavia (now named Jakarta) became the center of the Dutch empire in the East Indies. Later the Company settled and fortified the Cape of Good Hope, which served as a port of call on the long journey to the East. The power and prestige of the Company were completely unchallenged.

The Dutch were well aware of the possible existence of *Terra Australis,* which their maps showed as lying somewhere to the south of New Guinea. Their seamen made accidental and disconnected discoveries which, had they been followed up, might have changed the course of history. For it was during the early years of the East India Company that these Dutch mariners sighted and surveyed the northern, eastern, and, on one occasion, southern coasts of a land which was in fact Australia. For a time it was known as New Holland.

In 1611, a Dutch sea captain named Brouwer found a new and shorter route to the Indies by sailing due east from the Cape with the westerlies, and turning north, after 4,000 miles, to what was then Jacatra. Later expeditions followed this route and some were blown off course, being carried on to the coasts of a new land. In 1606, Willem Jansz had sailed his pinnace *Duyfken* (little dove) along the south coast of New Guinea, crossing to the eastern tip of northern Australia (now Cape York) and then sailing south into what is now the Gulf of Carpentaria as far as Cape Keer-weer (cape turn again). In 1616, Dirk Hartog in the *Eendracht* set up a pewter dish to mark his landing on Dirk Hartog Island off the west coast of an empty land which he named Eendrachtsland. In 1623, Jan Carstensz followed the *Duyfken's* route and explored the mainland, bringing back discouraging reports of barren land and savage black barbarians. In 1627, Peter Nuyts in the *Gulde Zeepaert* (golden seahorse) charted a portion of the south coast of New Holland, giving it the name of Nuytsland.

Surprisingly, however, it was not the East India Company that was responsible for the most daring and enterprising voyage of exploration in those adventurous years. That particular voyage came about as a direct challenge to the Company's authority. It was promoted by an Amsterdam merchant, Isaac le Maire, who had

Above: Jakob le Maire (1585–1616) who set out under his father's charter to trade in the Pacific. With the experienced pilot, Willem Schouten, as his sailing master, he made his way around South America and across the Pacific Ocean to the island of Java.

Left: the island of Tierra del Fuego is only about 1,000 miles north of Antarctica. Early natives of the island usually kept fires going for warmth. It was these fires that prompted Magellan to call the island Tierra del Fuego—"Land of Fire."

Right: Le Maire sighted the Horn Islands in 1616. His ship anchored in the bay and, after his men had scared the islanders by firing their guns as shown here, both sailors and islanders became friendly. For once no blood was shed during the visit. Exploring the islands the Dutch sailors saw no signs of cultivation.

This Uli figure from New Ireland is carved by the islanders from wood. The offspring of the figure are shown attached to his head and his legs.

obtained a charter to trade in the Pacific, provided that he did not trespass on the Company's traditional routes of access, the Cape of Good Hope and the Strait of Magellan. Undeterred by this apparently insurmountable handicap, Le Maire consulted with an experienced pilot named Willem Cornelis Schouten. They set themselves the task of locating a new passage into the Pacific, south of Magellan's, in the course of which they might discover whether Tierra del Fuego was a continent or an island. They thought it might even be feasible to search for the elusive continent mentioned in the memoirs of Quiros, some of which had fallen into Dutch hands.

At the end of May, 1615, the 220-ton *Eendracht* and the 110-ton *Hoorn* sailed from the island of Texel in The Netherlands. Commanding the expedition was Isaac le Maire's son Jakob, with Willem Cornelis Schouten as his sailing master. Captain of the *Hoorn* was Schouten's brother Jan. The ships called in at Sierra Leone on the west coast of Africa, exchanging "a few beads and some poor Nuremberg knives" for 25,000 lemons. This shrewd purchase helped to avert scurvy and to carry all but 3 of the 87-man crew safely through the 15-month voyage.

On December 8, the ships anchored at Port Desire in Patagonia.

Hoornse Insel.
Insula Horn.

The men saw ostriches, llamas, and the bones of an 11-foot "giant."
Here the *Hoorn* caught fire and was burned to cinders. Bypassing the
Strait of Magellan on January 24, 1616, the *Eendracht* entered a wide
strait with high land on either side. The land to the west was Tierra
del Fuego, which they renamed after Prince Maurice of Nassau.
The land to their east might be the Southern Continent itself, and
they named it Staten Island. It was, in fact, a small island off the Argen-
tinian coast. They saw sandy beaches, penguins and other sea birds,
and "whales by thousands," but found no anchorage. Leaving the
strait (later named for Le Maire), they sailed to the southwest, finding
themselves in deep blue water. They battled against heavy rollers
from the west—the Antarctic Drift—and on the evening of January
29 were astonished to see no more land ahead, only huge cliffs
looming above and stretching back to the north. It was the southern-
most tip of the American continent; they named it Cape Hoorn, after
their port of departure.

Steering a northerly course, the *Eendracht* reached the islands of
Juan Fernández and resumed the voyage to the northwest on March
3. Six days later Jan Schouten died at sea. On April 10, the ship's
crew landed briefly on a small coral island, where they came across

Carvings like this from New Ireland are
symbols used in memorial rites for the
dead, or initiation into manhood. The
preparation of carvings may take years
of skilled work.

three dogs but no sign of human occupation. Dog Island, as they called it, was probably Pukapuka in the Tuamotu group, first sighted by Magellan. Four days later they saw a fringe of land encircling a lagoon, and to this they gave the name Sonder Grondt (bottomless island). An atoll where they found fresh water they called Waterlandt, and another where they were attacked by swarms of flies they named Vliegen Eylandt (fly island). All these have been identified as part of the Tuamotu group.

On May 9, they sighted a double canoe carrying "red folk who smeared themselves with oil," and their island, where the *Eendracht* anchored next day, was named Cocos—actually Tafahi in the northern Tonga group. At another low island which the discoverers called Verraders (traitors') Island—present-day Niuatoputapu—they were lavishly supplied with coconuts, yams, bananas, chickens, and pigs.

On May 19, the *Eendracht* dropped anchor in the pleasant bay of a high island which, with its neighbor, they christened Hoornse Eylandten—now Futuna and Alofi in the Horn Islands, midway between Samoa and Fiji. The islanders were strongly built, intelligent people, with yellowish-brown skins. Their king was cooperative and for once there was no bloodshed. The Dutch entertained the natives with songs and dances, to the accompaniment of drums and trumpets, and the islanders returned the compliment. The visitors feasted on roast pork and fruits but could not be tempted to sample the potent home-made *kava*, a drink prepared from the root of the pepper plant. Apart from this the Dutch, as one of their company wrote, "got to be as free and easy there as if we had been at home." Le Maire felt sure they must be in the Solomon Islands and they tarried there for two weeks. Le Maire then proposed continuing westward in an effort to find Quiros' continent, but Schouten favored a safer course to the northwest towards the Moluccas.

The change of plan lost them the chance of rediscovering the real

Left: the Dutch East India Company built their headquarters at Batavia. The company's charter authorized them to import free of customs dues, maintain armed forces, erect forts and colonies, coin money, make treaties, and make war and peace.

Above: this map, from about 1670, shows the Indian Ocean and New Holland. The countries are beginning to have recognizably modern outlines on this map. But notice how narrow India appears, and how Australia and New Guinea almost meet.

Solomon Islands, though in the course of the voyage they did see and name a number of smaller islands. On June 25, they sighted the east coast of what was later called New Ireland, which they wrongly took to be New Guinea. On attempting to land they were assailed by coal-black islanders with rings in their noses. Some of the islanders were killed. A week later the explorers discovered the island subsequently known as New Hanover and several islands in the Admiralty group, one of which was named after Schouten. During July and August they sailed along the northern coast of New Guinea, arriving at Ternate in the Moluccas on September 17, and at Jacatra on October 28.

It had been a courageous and eventful voyage which had taken small toll of the lives either of the crew or of native populations. A new passage had been discovered into the Pacific, many new islands had been sighted for the first time, and unknown stretches of the New Guinea coastline had been accurately charted. But the Dutch East India Company was not prepared to countenance an expedition which had been organized as an act of sheer defiance. Governor General Coen charged Le Maire and Schouten with infringement of the Company's monopoly and refused to believe their story of a new route into the Pacific. The *Eendracht* was confiscated, and both men, together with 10 of their crew, were sent home with Joris van Spilbergen, then completing a round-the-world voyage. Le Maire, only 31, died on the way, a disillusioned man. But his father refused to let matters rest. He sued the East India Company, and after two years of legal wrangling succeeded in recovering both ship and cargo, together with costs, and establishing the existence of the strait bearing his name.

It was the Spanish who put the findings of this expedition to the test by sending out another, under the brothers Nodal. They

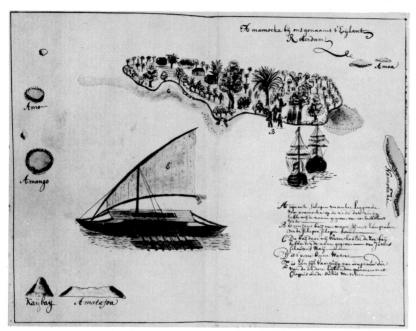

Left: early expeditions included artists who drew the strange sights explorers saw, to serve as a record. Incidents were also illustrated. This drawing shows Tasman's ships anchored off an island and being approached by natives in canoes.

rounded the Horn and returned by the Strait of Magellan, and thus proved Tierra del Fuego to be an island.

Another governor general of the East India Company, Anthony van Diemen, was responsible for organizing and inspiring the most celebrated of Dutch voyages of discovery, those of Abel Janszoon Tasman. But van Diemen's plans for a systematic and scientific survey of the southern Pacific were in turn based on the work of a brilliant navigator named Frans Jacobszoon Visscher. Visscher's *Memoir Concerning the Discovery of the South-land*, written in 1642, prompted the Company to dispatch an expedition which was intended to achieve one or more of several objectives. Although sections of the coast of New Holland had been charted, nobody knew if this was the Southern Continent itself. Neither did they know what relationship it bore to New Guinea, nor how far east and south it extended. Van Diemen planned that the expedition should sail to Mauritius in the Indian Ocean. From there they were to sail south until they reached latitude 54°. Then sailing east, they might reach *Terra Australis*, open up a new trade route to Chile, and even explore Le Maire Strait at the southern tip of South America. Even if the expedition discovered no land, argued Visscher, the ships could turn north to find the Solomon Islands and return via New Guinea.

Visscher sailed as chief navigator. The expedition set out on August 14, 1642, with instructions to find "the remaining unknown part of the terrestrial globe." Two ships, the *Heemskerck* and the *Zeehaen*, were provisioned for a year. Leader of the expedition was Abel Tasman, an employee of the Company, who, though he had valuable experience of navigating in the Indies, was efficient rather than brilliant. Visscher, far more imaginative yet no less practical,

In the 1640's, Abel Tasman, the Dutch navigator, sailed around the coast of Australia, showing that *Terra Australis* was an island continent. In honor of his discovery, the part of the Pacific Ocean washing the shores of eastern Australia is called the Tasman Sea.

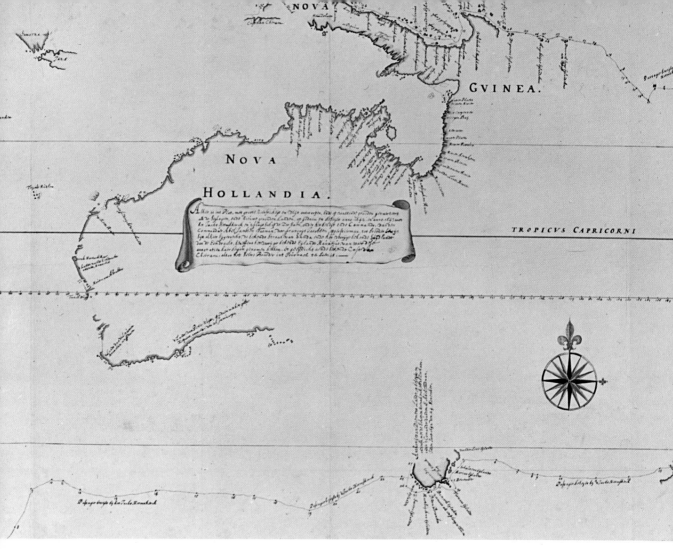

deserves as much credit as does Tasman for what the voyage achieved.

Tasman sailed from Batavia (formerly Jacatra) to Mauritius, where he was able to take on fresh provisions. Violent storms prevented their going as far south as they had planned. Nevertheless, they were far to the south of the normal trade route when they turned east. On November 24, they sighted land. They saw no inhabitants, nor did they attempt a landing, merely giving it the name of Van Diemen's Land. It was, in fact, the island later to bear Tasman's own name, Tasmania. Continuing eastward in the expectation of finding the "Salamonis Islands," they came across a desolate and rocky coastline on December 13. Some days later they encountered a group of half-naked, fierce-looking warriors in canoes, whose gestures were so menacing that Tasman decided not to linger. The land was given the name of Staten Land on the assumption that it was the western edge of the great Southern Continent, whose eastern coast had been found and similarly named by Le Maire. In fact, they had touched upon the south island of what later geographers called Nieuw Zeeland. The formidable warriors were Maoris.

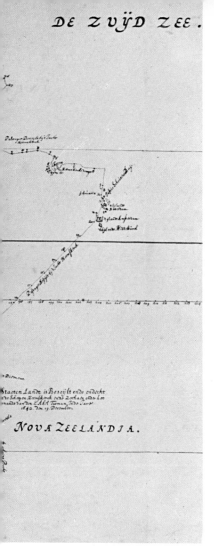

NOVA ZEELANDIA.

This map, which gives Tasman's routes and discoveries, is based on information gathered on his expeditions. It shows the northern coast of New Holland joining the coast of New Guinea. The map is part of the Blaeu Atlas, an atlas kept secret by the Dutch East India Company, so that competitors could not make use of the company's discoveries in the Pacific.

Tasman failed to establish what Cook later proved, that New Zealand consisted of two islands. Tasman did not realize that what he assumed was a deep inlet was actually a dividing strait. Thus he continued up the coast of the north island, setting course northeastwards on January 6, 1643. Within two weeks they were among the islands of the Tonga group, later renamed the Friendly Islands by Cook. The inhabitants certainly proved far more hospitable than the Maoris. The Dutch gave the islands such names as Middelburg (now Eua), Amsterdam (Tongatapu), and Rotterdam (Nomuka). The natives readily accepted old nails and knives in exchange for fresh water, fish, coconuts, fruit, pigs, and chickens.

Threading their way through dangerous reefs, the expedition soon came across several dozen islands that were not marked on their charts. Although they did not know it they were in the midst of the Fiji Islands, and were the first Europeans to visit them. But bad weather prevented any landing and they decided to follow in Le Maire's footsteps and make for Batavia via the familiar northern coast of New Guinea. If Visscher had been given his way, they would have sailed due west to rediscover the Torres Strait. As it was, they arrived back in Batavia on June 15, to a typically mournful Company reception. Tasman, in their view, "had been to some extent remiss in investigating the situation, conformation, and nature of the lands and peoples discovered."

The Company gave him another chance. On January 29, 1644, the *Limmen* and *Zeemeeuw* and the fishing boat *Bracq* sailed from Batavia. Once more Tasman had the benefit of Visscher's experience. This time they sailed along the southern coast of New Guinea, then south into the Gulf of Carpentaria. Finding no southern outlet they returned by way of the northern coast of New Holland, reaching Batavia in August. Again the Company expressed disapproval, accusing Tasman of having "found nothing that could be turned to profit, but . . . only naked, beach-roving wretches, destitute even of rice, miserably poor, and in many places of very bad disposition."

In 1645, the visionary Anthony van Diemen died. Tasman continued in the Company's employ, but made no more voyages. He eventually became a wealthy and respected landowner in Batavia, and died in 1659. There were to be no further grand designs by the Dutch. Tasman had encircled New Holland without being aware of it, and had shown that it did not stretch indefinitely eastward. What he discovered—and curiously, what he failed to discover—proved of considerable importance to those who followed him into the South Pacific, not least Captain James Cook.

It was almost 80 years before any Dutch explorer again ventured into the Pacific, and by that time the Dutch East India Company was no longer its former self. Profits were on the wane and The Netherlands' sea power was being challenged by both England and France. Political events in Europe during the second half of the 1600's curtailed further systematic exploration in the Pacific.

Below: in 1586, a single French buccaneer put the Spanish to flight and demanded—and received—a large sum of protection money from the port of Havana. Spanish ports and treasure ships were considered fair game by buccaneers, such as the Englishman William Dampier (right), as they cruised in the Caribbean Sea, and the Atlantic and Pacific oceans.

Buccaneers in the South Sea

Toward the end of the 1600's, the French and English buccaneers operating in the West Indies raided Spanish shipping and colonial possessions with impunity. Henry Morgan's capture of the city of Panamá in 1671—an enterprise which the diarist John Evelyn likened to the exploits of Drake—was followed by a replica of Drake's famous voyage, an English invasion of the Pacific. Meanwhile the naval power of The Netherlands was progressively sapped as a result of wars against England. The final straw was a war against France, known as the War of the Spanish Succession, in which England and The Netherlands joined forces. Although it resulted in the defeat of France, it nevertheless depleted the Dutch treasury and threatened her economy. The fortunes of her East India Company declined because of political developments at home.

The exploits of some of the most celebrated English buccaneers of the period—Bartholomew Sharp, John Coxon, Edmund Cook, Richard Hawkins, and others—do not form a part of our story of Pacific discovery. But among those who joined Coxon and Sharp in plundering the city of Panamá for a second time in 1680, and crossing the isthmus to raid the coast of Colombia, was an English adventurer named William Dampier. Although he was to participate in numerous buccaneering ventures, Dampier was no illiterate, bloodthirsty pirate, as were so many of his colleagues. He was, on the contrary, a highly intelligent man, drawn to a career of piracy mainly as a means of traveling and seeing new places and peoples. A contemporary described him as "the mildest mannered man that ever scuttled ship or cut a throat." He was also a writer of considerable merit. His journals, first recounting his experiences in the South Seas and later his voyage round the world, make absorbing reading.

Dampier and his surgeon friend Lionel Wafer parted company with Sharp on April 17, 1681, and struggled back, with a small party, across the isthmus and later to Virginia. But the lure of the South Seas enticed Dampier back for another buccaneering voyage in a stolen Danish vessel, which was renamed the *Batchelor's Delight*. A stormy passage round Cape Horn in February, 1684, took the ship into the Pacific, poised to strike at the silver galleons bound from Chile and Peru for Panama. The following year they were joined by the *Cygnet*, commanded by Captain Charles Swan. The two ships, though well armed, met with only moderate success. Dampier later left Edward Davis, captain of the *Batchelor's Delight*,

Storms at sea are always unpleasant.
But for the early explorers in their small
sailing ships a storm could be fatal.
They could be blown off course so that
they drifted, lost in an empty sea, until
they died of hunger and thirst. Their
ship could be so damaged that it sank
before they reached land. This
illustration shows Dampier and some
of his companions in a small native
canoe, being tossed in a storm.

Right: silver, mined by the Spanish in newly-discovered Peru and Chile, made Spanish galleons attractive prey to roving British buccaneers.

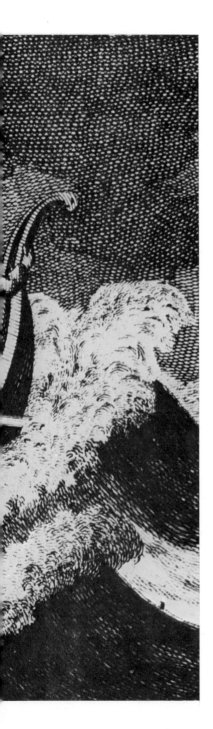

to join Swan in the *Cygnet*. It would appear that he was disillusioned with buccaneering and believed Swan was preparing to probe more deeply into the Pacific, a prospect which appealed greatly to his questing nature. So he was no longer a crew member of the *Batchelor's Delight* when, in 1687, Davis sighted an island, some 1,500 miles west of Chile, in latitude 27° 20′, which he named Davis Land. It was later suggested that this may have been Easter Island, but nothing in the description, apart from the latitude, tallies.

Dampier and Swan, meanwhile, had crossed the Pacific in the *Cygnet*, leaving Cape Corrientes in Mexico on March 31, 1686, and reaching Guam in 51 days—a voyage of 7,300 miles. They continued their journey to Mindanao in the Philippine Islands where they stayed for over six months. The crew were generally dissatisfied with Captain Swan and finally mutinied. They left him and 36 of the crew ashore and sailed away. Dampier went with the mutineers and took the *Cygnet* on a leisurely voyage through the Spice Islands and eventually down to the northwest coast of New Holland. There the ship was overhauled and Dampier became the first Englishman to set foot in Australia. But his reports were no more enthusiastic than those of the Dutchmen who had preceded him. The Aborigines, he considered, "were the miserablest people in the world."

Dampier soon tired of his comrades on the *Cygnet* and escaped from them in the Nicobar Islands, crossing the Indian Ocean with seven companions in a canoe and arriving home, after many adventures, in the autumn of 1691. He learned later that the *Cygnet* had capsized off Madagascar, with heavy loss of life.

In 1697, Dampier published his journals under the title of *A New Voyage Around the World*. His graphic descriptions of the Pacific not only made him money but spurred the government to authorize an English voyage of discovery to search for the mysterious *Terra Australis*. On January 14, 1699, Dampier sailed in the 292-ton *Roebuck*. The ship was small and rotting, the crew surly and incompetent. Taking the Cape of Good Hope route, they sighted the west coast of New Holland on July 31. The *Roebuck* cruised north along the bleak shoreline for five weeks. Then, after naming a stretch of it Dampier Land, the former buccaneer and his crew headed north toward Timor. Continuing past the islands bordering the western tip of New Guinea, he reached the island of New Hanover. Hugging

A group of three small islands off the coast of Chile were discovered in 1563 by a pilot, Juan Fernández, a Portuguese in Spanish service. He gave the little island group his own name.

the coasts, he sailed round two larger islands—New Ireland and New Britain. To all three, which appeared to be joined, he gave the name New Britain, reporting that it had pleasant wooded landscapes and friendly inhabitants. He then took the *Roebuck* through the passage separating New Britain and New Guinea, which he named Dampier Strait. He journeyed back along the way he had come, but this time closer to the New Guinea coastline. He returned to Timor, and from there to Batavia. The rotten state of the ship and his unreliable crew forced Dampier to hurry home. By February, 1701, he had reached Ascension Island in the South Atlantic. There the rotting hull of the *Roebuck* gave up altogether and the ship sank. The crew was later rescued by another British ship.

Dampier had already sailed round the world once, though it had taken him many years and he had traveled aboard several different vessels. He was to repeat the feat twice more, in 1703–1707 and in 1708–1711, the last time as pilot of Woodes Rogers' *Duke* on another privateering venture. He was more in his element this time probably because he was a better navigator than commander. The *Duke* sailed round the Horn and rescued a Scottish sailor named Alexander Selkirk from what was later called Róbinson Crusoe Island in the Juan Fernández group. Selkirk had been marooned there for four years,

The *Cinque Ports*, a ship which accompanied Dampier on part of his third voyage, stopped at the Juan Fernández Islands in 1704, and while there, the captain quarrelled with his quartermaster, who was marooned on one of the islands. In 1709 Dampier returned and rescued the quartermaster, Alexander Selkirk. The English author, Daniel Defoe, heard about Selkirk's adventures, and wrote his famous book about a man shipwrecked on an isolated island, *Robinson Crusoe*.

and his experience provided Daniel Defoe with material for *Robinson Crusoe*. Rogers continued up the South American coast, raiding Guayaquil, and capturing 14 Spanish ships, but not the long sought treasure galleon on its way to Manila. After returning home via Guam and the Indies, Dampier retired on the proceeds of three books. The lively accounts of the places and people he had encountered, however, opened the eyes of his countrymen to the legitimate commercial possibilities of the South Seas, and provided added impetus for the later voyages of Cook,

When Jacob Roggeveen sighted icebergs near Cape Horn in 1721 he thought they were the outlying edges of the supposed great Southern Continent for which explorers were still looking.

The Last Dutch Voyage

9

In the 1720's, the Dutch enjoyed their last fling in the Pacific. In 1621, the Dutch West India Company had been formed. By the end of the century it promised to be more enterprising and profitable even than the East India Company. It was to the West India Company, therefore, that in 1696 a gentleman named Roggeveen submitted a new proposal for the discovery of southern lands. With The Netherlands practically bankrupt, he could hardly have chosen a worse time, and he was not surprisingly turned down. When he died, he made his son Jacob promise to revive the project at some more opportune moment. Jacob Roggeveen was a lawyer who rose to high office in the service of the East India Company and retired with a fortune. He was no longer a young man when, in 1721, he made overtures to the West India Company, which agreed to finance an expedition to the South Pacific.

Three ships were fitted out, the *Arend*, the *Thienhoven*, and the *Africaansche Galey*, and Roggeveen sailed from the island of Texel on August 21, 1721. The ships rounded the Horn in appalling weather. Immense icebergs were sighted in latitude 62° 30′. Roggeveen felt that these must be the outposts of the reputed *Terra Australis* or Southern Continent, stretching to the Pole, but the combination of violent winds, thick fog, impenetrable snow and hail, and rough seas was too much for the ships. They were forced to turn north until they reached Juan Fernández Islands. As English buccaneers had already hinted, these islands seemed to be an excellent base for privateering raids and suitable for settlement as well. Roggeveen decided to look further into these possibilities on his return, confident that it was "the best laid scheme for promoting southern discoveries that ever yet entered the head of man."

Roggeveen assumed that *Terra Australis* must lie somewhere between latitude 30° and 36°, but chose first to follow up the vague report circulated by the Englishman Edward Davis, who, 34 years earlier, claimed to have sighted "Davis Land" in latitude 27° 20′ S—some 1,500 miles from Chile. He failed to find any land in the area and concluded that the English buccaneers must have been "rovers from truth as well as rovers after the goods of the Spaniards." But on April 5, 1722, Easter Sunday, land was indeed sighted—not the great continent, but a small island. Smoke rose from points along the shore, and from a distance it appeared to be green and fertile, with many trees and undulating hills. Roggeveen named the island Easter Island, and so it has remained to this day.

Next morning an islander clambered aboard the *Arend*, and strolled up and down the deck. Suddenly he scared himself by glimpsing his reflection in a mirror, and swam back to shore. Other islanders went aboard and stole some sailors' caps and Roggeveen's table cloth. In the afternoon Roggeveen took a strong landing party ashore. Inexplicably, some of them opened fire and killed a number of the islanders. But the episode seemed to have no adverse effect, and during the week that the Dutch lay offshore, relations with the islanders remained friendly.

Easter Island was 2,400 miles from Chile and 1,500 from the nearest inhabited island. How the islanders reached their isolated home, and where they had come from, has never been discovered. Unfortunately, Roggeveen, who was in the best position to find out, gave little more than a cursory inspection to the most remarkable feature of the island—the huge statues, standing on stone platforms, which lined the shore, with their backs to the sea. Some of them were over 30 feet tall and were reckoned to weigh more than 50 tons. All the figures had elongated heads, some on foreshortened trunks, with the same extended ears as the islanders themselves. A number of them were topped by immense cylindrical "hats," which Roggeveen described as baskets containing red stones, but which might have been intended to represent topknots of hair, again modeled on the islanders' styles. Roggeveen guessed that the statues were made of clay, which crumbled between the fingers, reinforced by smooth pebbles. But there is no record of his asking the islanders how they came to be there. Later explorers showed that the construction material was compressed volcanic *tuff* or ash.

Although the Dutch visitors saw the islanders light fires in front of the statues and squat before them, raising and lowering their

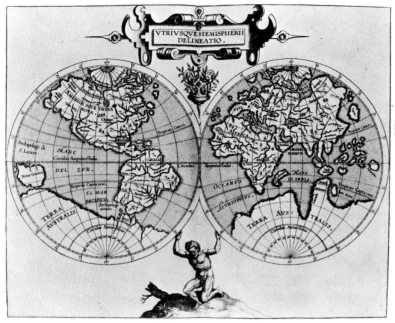

Left: this world map of the 1700's shows *Terra Australis* as Roggeveen assumed it existed, stretching across the globe from the tropics to the Pole.

Left: Roggeveen said in his log, "we noticed that they kindle fire in front of certain remarkable tall stone figures they set up; and, thereafter squatting on their heels with heads bowed down, they bring the palms of the hands together and alternatively raise and lower them. We could not understand how it was possible that people who are destitute of heavy or thick timber . . . had been able to erect them; nevertheless some of these statues were a good 30 feet in height and broad in proportion."

hands as if in prayer, they did not pause to consider the possible significance of this. It was left to later explorers to wonder how such huge figures were built and transported to their sites, and to make a thorough investigation of their nature and distribution.

The Easter Islanders were strong and well built. Their skins were yellowish to light brown and were freely tattooed with blue paint. Some of the inhabitants were long-haired, others had short hair and beards. Their clothes were not woven but appeared to be made of vegetable material. The most unusual and striking of their physical features were their abnormally long ears, the lobes pulled down almost to shoulder level and pierced to hold large, heavy, ornamental rings. Roggeveen was not impressed by their canoes, which seemed flimsy and leaked badly. Their huts were very simple, branches and grass covering a thin framework. The islanders were well provided with fruits and vegetables—including sweet potatoes —and with sugar cane and poultry. They lacked cooking utensils, roasting their chickens by wrapping them in grass and leaves and placing them on heated stones.

Found on Easter Island, this stone is decorated with a painting of a birdman. It was probably part of a bird cult, an important part of island life.

Below: the coastline of Makatea, which Roggeveen called Refreshment Island. Below left: Easter Islanders today have preserved many of the skills of their ancestors, such as this traditional way of cooking food by placing it in an earth pit with hot stones. Normally, they live a relatively civilized life, their major difficulty being their isolation from the established shipping channels. Their main contact with the outside world is the regular supply ship which comes from Chile.

Roggeveen seems to have been relieved to see the last of this fascinating island. He had long abandoned his search for the Southern Continent and continued on a more or less parallel course to that taken by Le Maire and Schouten. There were islands in plenty, so tightly clustered in the Tuamotu group that he named them the Labyrinth. The *Africaansche Galey* was wrecked on a reef near one of these, which Roggeveen named Schadelijk (disastrous)—now Takapoto, Le Maire's "bottomless island."

On June 2, they landed at Verkwikking (refreshment) Island, now Makatea, still in the Tuamotu Islands. Here a landing party was ambushed and showered with stones, and 10 men died. Others on board were dying of scurvy, and provisions were running short. Roggeveen had clearly lost his zeal for further adventure, and decided to make directly for the East Indies. They sighted Bora Bora and Maupiti in the Society Islands, then various atolls in the Samoa group. The fair-skinned, tattooed islanders seemed friendly, but the crew was in too poor a shape now to linger. Back they sailed, north of the Solomon Islands and New Guinea, through the Moluccas to Batavia, arriving at the end of September, 1722. Here the East India Company impounded Roggeveen's ships, indignant at his having trespassed on their territory. They sent him and his surviving crew members home as virtual captives. Such was the inglorious end of the last of the Dutch expeditions in the Pacific.

The Circum-navigators

10

The 1700's saw the new colonial powers of England and France in conflict in many parts of the world—on either side of the Atlantic, in the Indian Ocean, and in the Pacific. The voyages of Tasman, Roggeveen, Dampier, and the buccaneers had kept alive the magnetic appeal of *Terra Australis*. The governments of both nations were urged to lose no opportunity of seeking out the riches which indisputably lay in store for those bold enough to go out and find them. In England, John Campbell reissued John Harris' *Book of Voyages*, originally published in 1705, pleading for commercial exploitation of the great Southern Continent. The new edition coincided with the return of Captain, later Admiral, George Anson from his circumnavigation of the world in the *Centurion* between 1740 and 1744. Anson's voyage was in fact a disastrous one, for he managed to lose five of his six ships and more than 1,050 men out of 1,955, mostly from scurvy. The passage round Cape Horn was

Above: George Anson (1697–1762) started his voyage around the world in 1740. Ten years afterward he was made First Lord of the Admiralty and introduced reforms that raised the British navy to high efficiency.

catastrophic, and was only partially redeemed by the capture of a Manila galleon off the Philippine Islands, with booty worth millions of dollars. But the account of Anson's voyage appealed to the public just as powerfully as the semifictional narrative of *Robinson Crusoe*, published back in 1719.

In the course of Anson's gale-swept passage round the Horn, one of his ships, the *Wager*, was wrecked on the rocks off the coast of Chile. One of the rescued crew members was a 17-year-old midshipman named John Byron, later known, because of his seemingly endless encounters with rough seas, as "Foul Weather Jack." His vivid *Narrative of the Hon. John Byron* told the incredible story of his 4½-year journey back to England. It included a year of living among the islanders, ill-treatment by Indians, imprisonment by the Spaniards, and enforced shipment to France. Nineteen years later, in the summer of 1764, Byron sailed again as captain of the frigate

Left: many of the early explorers kept journals which they illustrated. This charming picture of a seal illustrates the journal of a man who sailed with George Anson.

Lyons & Seals, they are both Amphibious, & something alike excepting their Size and some few other differences; the Noise they make, together with the continual Cry of the Dogs, the Murmuring of the Runs of Fresh Water, with the Surf beating on the Rocks, & the appearance of the Land makes a Romantick but very agreeable Scene.

The Sea Lyon is a large Animal the Head of the Female something like a Lyon, from whence I imagine it takes its Name, the Male has a large Trunk or Snout hanging over his face like that of an Elephant, they are generally between Twenty & thirty feet Long, Cover'd with Short Hair & Larger than any two Oxen I ever saw; they have two finns or rather hands on their sides, and there Tails either when angerd or in the Water part into four Finns more, which are of great use to them in Swimming, they wade on the shore very fast by the help of their Paws; they are so much the Colour and lye so like a Rock until they are Rous'd, that I have frequently mistaken them until I have almost Stumbled on them as they lay single among the Rocks; they generally

Above: like other explorers heading for the Pacific, John Byron landed in Patagonia, an area near the southern tip of South America on the Atlantic coast. The local Indians wore large boots stuffed with straw. The first visitors, who were Spanish, named them *patagones* "big feet."

Below: weapons in the Pacific could be vicious. This dagger from the Gilbert Islands has sharks' teeth on the curved blade for ragged slashing.

Dolphin, with 190 officers and men. It was a sturdy ship, its rudder sheathed in copper, a forerunner of later copper-bottomed vessels. With the *Dolphin* sailed the sloop *Tamar*, with a crew of 115. The *Tamar* was commanded by Captain Patrick Mount and the first lieutenant was young Philip Carteret.

Byron's voyage was ostensibly a trip to the East Indies, but its primary objective was to survey the South Atlantic, particularly the Falkland Islands and Pepys Island, thought to lie in the vicinity. The Falkland Islands were regarded as a useful base for access to the Pacific. It was of paramount importance to the English to lay claim to the Falkland Islands before the French did, and the French were known to be thinking along the same lines. Byron was then to proceed to Drake's New Albion and resume the search for a North-west Passage.

The voyage, however, did not go according to this plan. The two ships reached Port Desire, on the Patagonian coast, in late November. In the New Year they surveyed the Falkland Islands, naming the various capes and bays and claiming them for the British Crown. Byron satisfied himself that Pepys Island was a figment of the imagination, and then sailed through the Strait of Magellan. On the way he passed a French ship, not realizing that it was bound for the Falkland Islands where a French settlement was established.

Emerging into the Pacific on April 9, 1765, Byron altered his plans. Not for him the icy waters of a possibly non-existent North-west Passage. His destination was the Solomon Islands. Unable to anchor at Napuka or Tepoto in the Tuamotu Islands group, he named them the Islands of Disappointment. Two days later he dropped anchor off Takaroa, and christened it and its neighbor Takapoto the King George Islands. The friendly islanders offered coconuts, but not, as the voyagers hoped, pearls. The seamen came across a

wormeaten rudder, evidently from Roggeveen's wrecked *Afric-aansche Galey*. Other islands in the area they named after the royal family, except for Byron Island in the Gilbert group, which they sighted on July 2. The copper-colored islanders of this region had elongated ears and were naked apart from shell ornaments. They were friendly but of a thievish disposition. By now Byron's enthusiasm for discovery had waned. He had not found the Solomon Islands. Food and water were low, but fortunately coconuts provided a surprising remedy for scurvy. On July 31, the two ships reached Tinian in the Mariana Islands, arriving back in England on May 9, 1766, after a singularly unproductive round-the-world voyage.

Within four months the *Dolphin*, completely refitted, was at sea again, commanded this time by Captain Samuel Wallis. Wallis was a cautious and considerate man, but unfortunately not in the best of health. This time the objective of the voyage was undisguisedly the Southern Continent. The ship carried provisions and medical supplies for a long voyage, including three hundredweight of soup as a protection against scurvy. The second vessel, the sloop *Swallow*, commanded by Philip Carteret, was in a disgraceful condition, old, rickety, and quite unsuitable for a voyage of this nature. Carteret accepted the command hoping that he would be able to exchange her for a copper-sheathed frigate in the Falkland Islands.

Carteret received no replacement vessel and the passage through the Strait of Magellan was a nightmare. That the *Swallow* survived at all was little short of a miracle. When the ships emerged after a four-month battle against gales, she was left far behind. The *Dolphin* continued on a northwesterly course, finding it impossible to sail due west. There was scurvy despite a strict diet that included the soup and pickled cabbage. Various islands in the Tuamotu group were named for members of the royal family. Then on June 18, 1767,

Below: the native Tahitians were so friendly to Captain Wallis and his crew that it was difficult for the ship to weigh anchor among the canoes.

Above: the tales of returning sailors of the beauty of the islands and the friendliness of the people gave Tahiti the name "Paradise of the Pacific."

Below: as elsewhere, the Tahitians had their weapons, which included slings, spears, and these business-like axes.

a larger island loomed up on the horizon. When the mist cleared next morning the *Dolphin* was surrounded by hundreds of canoes. The islanders swarmed aboard. One of them was butted by the ship's goat. The shock drove the astonished islander and his companions overboard, but they had already taken various souvenirs.

Although Wallis was ill, even he could hardly conceal his delight at the beauty of the island whose coast they skirted for four days in search of anchorage. This was no barren atoll but a well inhabited and fertile land, worthy of dedication to the king. So after dropping anchor in the tree-fringed Matavai Bay, Wallis went ashore, hoisted the flag and gave it the name of King George the Third Island. Later explorers knew it better as Tahiti, largest of the group named by Cook as the Society Islands.

Initially the islanders proved hostile. Parties looking for water were pelted with stones by the men and with fruit by the women. Once the ship's guns had to be fired as a warning when thousands of islanders paddled out in canoes. These, however, were the only dangerous incidents, and no lives were lost. Wallis and his men gradually gained the confidence of the islanders. Reconnaissance

AREAREA

parties led by Furneaux, the second lieutenant, confirmed that this was a singularly lovely island, with hills and mountains, trees, rivers, and green valleys and groves. The climate was delightful, the villages clean and well stocked with fruits, fish, and meat, including pork, duck, and dog flesh. Food was cooked in pits on hot embers and stones. The islanders had stone axes and were clearly expert boat-builders. Wallis saw great ceremonial double canoes as well as simple dugouts and single outriggers. Clubs, spears, and slings appeared to be the standard weapons, with bows and arrows used only for hunting.

The people themselves were very attractive. The men were well-built and handsome, and liberally tattooed. The women were particularly alluring. Both sexes wore clothing made of tree bark and decked themselves freely with shell, pearl, flower, and bird-feather ornaments. The women's standards of morality were far removed from those expected of the wives and daughters who had been left at home. They seemed to prize nails above all other objects of barter and the more hot-blooded crew members almost wrecked the ship in their eagerness to obtain the women's attentions. Finally, Wallis

One of the important contributions to Tahiti's fame was the work of the French artist, Paul Gauguin. He spent the last years of his life on the island and painted some of his finest pictures there. This painting, called "Arearea" was one that helped to give Tahiti its romantic reputation.

observed: "To preserve the ship from being pulled to pieces, I ordered that no man, except the wooders and waterers, with their guard, should be permitted to go on shore." These precautions were not enough to deter the bolder spirits who considered a flogging a small price to pay for the delights offered by the island maidens. Wallis, however, strongly denied subsequent accusations that it was his men who introduced venereal disease to Tahiti. Wallis himself said he saw no sign of any form of disease, not even malaria.

Once Wallis and his first lieutenant were fit enough, they were brought ashore and entertained by the local chieftainess or queen, a tall, stout woman named Purea. She proved herself strong enough on one occasion to lift Wallis over some puddles and insisted that he submit to a massage performed by four of her maidservants. The ship's surgeon astonished the islanders by removing his wig because of the heat.

The visitors spent several pleasant weeks in these idyllic surroundings, and they contributed to the local vegetation by planting lemon, lime, and orange pips and plum, peach, and cherry stones. When the time came for them to leave, the queen seemed genuinely grief-stricken. After an exchange of presents, the *Dolphin* sailed on July 27. Moorea in the Society group was named after the Duke of York and so many smaller islands were discovered that Wallis ran out of royal names and had to start on distinguished officers of the navy. A group including Uvea, north of Tonga, he claimed for himself as the Wallis Islands.

To Wallis' credit, not a single man died on this, the most rewarding and trouble-free of Pacific voyages. On May 20, 1768, the *Dolphin* was back home, her captain eager to recount the marvels of the idyllic South Sea island he had discovered.

Meanwhile, Philip Carteret was laboring across the stormy

Above: when Philip Carteret first saw Pitcairn Island in 1767, it was uninhabited. The first people to live there were the mutineers from the British ship, the *Bounty,* who found its isolated position a perfect refuge. The 6 sailors brought with them 12 Tahitian women, and established a small community. Today most of their descendants have moved to Norfolk Island, far to the west, but a few of the families still live on Pitcairn.

Left: the island of Tahiti is rich with vegetation. The islanders have found a use for almost everything that grows around them. Some of the plants are edible, some are used in the making of clothes and houses, and some provide bright color dyes.

Pacific, his *Swallow* bruised and battered, her crew weak with scurvy, her whereabouts unknown. Carteret tried to reassure his men with brave words, promising them "that although the *Dolphin* was the best ship, I did not doubt that I should find more than equivalent advantages in their courage, ability and good conduct." It says much for his qualities that he managed to drag the *Swallow* across the ocean safely to port.

Carteret's first shock was to find the Juan Fernández Islands fortified by the Spanish. Continuing north and then west the crew sighted only a tiny rock island, which they named Pitcairn after the young officer who first spotted it. They also named islands in the Tuamotu group. Still the ship was plagued by foul weather and disease. At last the *Swallow* fell in with the trade winds and on August 12, 1767, with morale at its lowest ebb and the ship leaking alarmingly, they came upon an island group which Carteret named Queen Charlotte Islands. He later learned that the islands were the Santa Cruz group. Here the very dark-skinned, curly-haired islanders gave his men an even more hostile reception than that given to

South Sea Islanders use many of
nature's wonders that grow around
them to make beautiful jewelry and
ornaments. This ornament from the
Santa Cruz Islands is made from
shell with a tortoiseshell overlay.

Mendaña and Quiros two centuries earlier. The ship's master
returned from a foray with three arrows sticking into him. He died,
together with three of his party, having paid a cruel price for dis-
obeying orders by firing on the islanders, and ruining all chance of
friendly cooperation and replenishment of provisions.

After leaving Santa Cruz and beating off an attack by the islanders,
Carteret changed course and by sheer accident found himself,
although he did not realize it, among the Solomon Islands. He failed
to recognize the islands for what they were and dared not stay to
investigate. Off Ndai, which Carteret named Gower Island after his
first lieutenant, the crew captured a canoe full of coconuts. Then
they named another island Carteret Island (now Malaita). On
August 26, the *Swallow* sailed into St. George Bay, visited by Dampier
in 1700. Carteret found it was not a bay but a strait dividing two
large islands. To the south was Dampier's New Britain. The island
to the north they renamed New Ireland. In a nearby cove they
patched up the ship, collected fresh coconuts, and took aboard fresh
water. Then, passing through the strait, Carteret named a third
island New Hanover. Other small islands in the vicinity he named
the Admiralty Islands. They were clearly well wooded and populated, but Carteret did not pause to make acquaintance with the
naked islanders with their white-streaked faces. He pressed on,
charting islands on the way, sailing parallel to the north coast of
New Guinea, up to Mindanao, then south down the west coast of
Celebes to Macassar. It was now December, and half his crew were
dead or dying. They landed in Macassar, but the occupying Dutch
almost provoked an armed clash and the crew were unable to repair
the *Swallow* until they reached Batavia five months later. These
repairs took another four months and it was not until March, 1769,
that the expedition reached England, after a round-the-world
voyage lasting 31 months. For sheer determination and courage the
voyage is second to none in the annals of seafaring.

On the last lap, somewhere in mid-Atlantic, the *Swallow* had been
overtaken by a French frigate. The officer who came on board
seemed familiar with the ship and her exploits and questioned
Carteret closely about his experiences. Carteret would give no
details, and sent the man away with a present of a Santa Cruz arrow
for his captain. This vessel was none other than *La Boudeuse* (the
sulky woman), commanded by Louis-Antoine de Bougainville,

which had followed Carteret across the Pacific and was herself on the last leg of her trip round the world. Carteret discovered her mission too late for "though the French ship was foul after a long voyage, and we had just been cleaned, she shot by us as if we had been at anchor, notwithstanding we had a fine fresh gale and all our sails set." Bougainville was quite accurate in describing the *Swallow* as "very small, went very ill, and when we took leave of him, he remained as it were at anchor. How much he must have suffered in so bad a vessel may well be conceived."

Bougainville himself was more than a great explorer in his own right. He had served against the British with Montcalm at Quebec, written a mathematical treatise, and made his mark as a scientist, diplomat, and writer. From the pages of his *Voyage Round the World* emerges a figure of great charm and humanity. Patriotism, coupled with a natural flair for adventure, had led him in 1764 to found a French settlement in the Falkland Islands, which his government regarded as strategically vital for exploration and trade. But after the British had staked their claim it was decided to enlist Spain's support in the war against England by selling the colony. Bougainville was

Bougainville visited the Falkland Islands which are so close to the Antarctic that penguins thrive there. The French navigator saw three species and comments in his journal, "We hoped to be able to bring one of them over to Europe. It was easily tamed so far as to follow and know the person that had the care of feeding it."

ordered to hand it over in person and to extend the journey to the colony into a full-scale search for the Southern Continent.

Bougainville took two ships, the newly built, 32-gun frigate *La Boudeuse*, with a 230-man crew, and the store ship *Etoile* (star). The scientific manner in which this expedition was planned distinguished it from all its predecessors. On board were the botanist Philibert de Commerson and a young astronomer named Véron. Also on board, unknown to Bougainville, was a young valet, later unmasked by the ship's surgeon as Commerson's mistress, Jeanne Baret, to whom went the honor of becoming the first woman to sail round the world!

Bougainville sailed from Nantes in France on November 15, 1766, and anchored in Montevideo harbor at the end of January. In April he sailed to the Falkland Islands and handed them over to the Spanish. It was a year before the exploratory part of the voyage began. Then it took 52 days to negotiate the Strait of Magellan. On January 26, 1768, the two ships headed toward Davis Land.

Bougainville, like Roggeveen and Carteret, concluded it did not exist. On March 22, they spotted four small islands in the Tuamotu group, part of the treacherous Labyrinth. Refusing to believe that they could form any part of a Southern Continent, Bougainville sagely remarked: "I agree that it is difficult to conceive such a number of low islands, and almost drowned lands, without supposing a continent near it. But Geography is a science of facts; in studying it, authors must by no means give way to any system, formed in their studies, unless they would run the risk of being subject to very great errors, which can be rectified only at the expense of navigators." This system was precisely what stay-at-home discoverers had been indulging in for many centuries.

The weather now turned nasty, and scurvy began to attack the crew despite the lemon juice and distilled water provided to prevent it. Happily, on April 2, they saw the peak of Mehetea, already discovered by Wallis, and shortly afterwards, Otaheite—now Tahiti. On the morning of April 4, *La Boudeuse* was surrounded by canoes laden with fruit, and full of handsome men and beautiful women. Two days later the ship anchored in the Hitiaa lagoon, well east of the bay where the *Dolphin* had lain. The north coast of the island was as lush and beautiful as the south, the islanders as hospitable—in every

Right: mangoes were one of the new fruits tasted by explorers when they visited the Pacific Islands. The mango tree can grow as tall as 50 feet and the long pointed leaves as long as 12 inches. The fruit itself has a thick skin, with the delicious flesh clinging to a flat, fibrous pip.

sense—as before. Though there was no sign of Queen Purea, the local chieftain Ereti was as friendly as she had been. Gifts were exchanged—nails, buttons, and cloth in return for the island's choicest fruits and vegetables.

The French were more lyrical about the island and its inhabitants than the prosaic British. It was their extravagant praises that built up in Europe the legend of a South Seas paradise where the "noble savage" lived in a state of blissful innocence. Bougainville claimed the island for France and named it New Cythera, unaware that Wallis

The shrub Bougainvillea, found in the Pacific Islands and in South America, was named for Bougainville. It is a climbing plant that grows to a height of 10 feet or more, producing bright flowers of red or purple.

had forestalled him. He suspected that it was not as idyllic as it seemed. He heard reports of tribal feuds, ritual murder, and killing of unwanted infants, which seemed to bear out his more cautious judgment. Nevertheless, his 10-day visit was a pleasant interlude. He left behind some grains and seeds, and allowed Commerson to give the name Bougainvillea to a beautiful local climbing plant. Then, to a chorus of weeping island women, *La Boudeuse* put to sea again, taking the chieftain's brother Ahutoru back to Europe.

Setting a westward course, the sailors sighted and named various islands in the Samoa and New Hebrides groups. Then they saw Espiritu Santo. Here Bougainville made an important decision. Previous explorers had played safe and struck northwest. Bougainville, still curious about the land that lay to the west and ignorant of Torres' findings, decided to sail due west. He suspected that Santo might be linked with New Holland as part of the Southern Continent. But on June 4, he ran into heavy breakers and two days later was forced by a continuous line of rocks and reefs to change course to the northeast. Had Bougainville but known, he was no more than a hundred miles from the unknown east coast of New Holland, on the fringes of the Great Barrier Reef. His duty, however, was to get

a rapidly weakening crew back to safety. The shortage of food drove some of the men to eat rats.

On June 10, the crew sighted the pleasant, southern coast of New Guinea. But the weather was so bad that the ship risked breaking up on the reefs. At last, on June 20, the expedition rounded the tip of the Louisiade Archipelago to which Bougainville thankfully gave the apt name of Cape Deliverance. Continuing northward, he failed to realize that he was among the Solomon Islands. Even when he published his book in 1771 Bougainville did not place them accurately jotting down the note ". . . whose existence and positions are doubtful." The islanders of the region were so obviously hostile that Bougainville decided to make for New Britain after naming Choiseul for the Duc de Choiseul and Bougainville Island for himself. Reaching New Britain on July 7, 1768, they found wood and water but no fruit or fish. They saw signs of Carteret's expedition of the previous year, then decided to make as quickly as possible for the safety of the Moluccas. They were attacked by islanders from New Ireland. Scurvy and semistarvation added to their ordeals. Yet morale was maintained by holding dances on deck every evening. Crawling along the north coast of New Guinea, Bougainville

On the homeward leg of his voyage around the world, Bougainville sailed along the coast of New Guinea. Native canoes, like this one with the sail folded on top of the cabin, went out to the ships and the islanders tried to attack them with stones and arrows.

glumly remarked: "People have long argued about the location of hell. Frankly, we have discovered it."

At Batavia, which they reached on September 28, news was received of Wallis and Carteret. The latter had left only 12 days previously. Bougainville overtook him in the Atlantic and anchored off St. Malo on March 16, 1769, after the first French circumnavigation of the world.

One victim of the journey was Ahutoru, the chieftain's brother. For a while he was the idol of Paris society. He became fond of

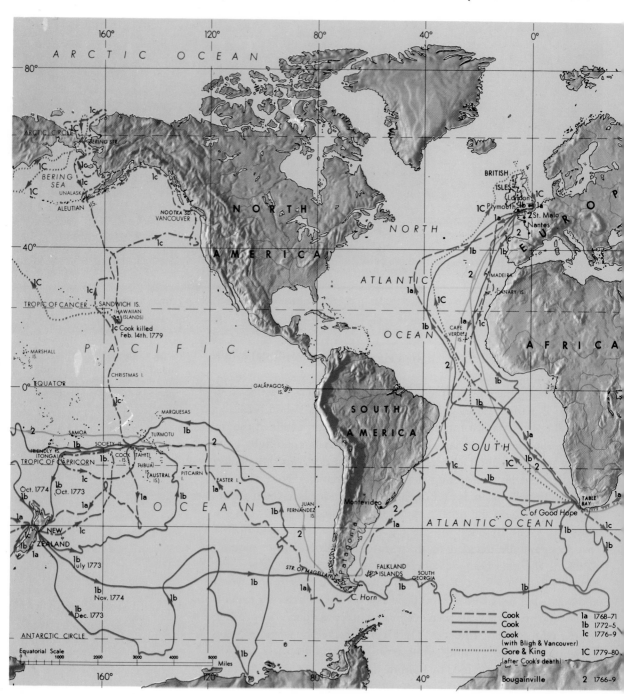

Cook	1a 1768–71
Cook	1b 1772–5
Cook (with Bligh & Vancouver)	1c 1776–9
Gore & King (after Cook's death)	1C 1779–80
Bougainville	2 1766–9

French wine and food, and cultivated a taste for ballet. But he yearned for home, and Bougainville spent a large sum of money to get him shipped back. On the way Ahutoru died of smallpox.

On the day that Bougainville arrived home, Lieutenant James Cook of the Royal Navy was already in the Pacific and bound for Tahiti. It was the first of three voyages that were to eclipse everything that had gone before, both in the scope of their discoveries and in their contributions to science. The final pages of Pacific exploration awaited only his writing of them.

The voyages of Captain Cook. This map also shows the course followed by Gore and King after Cook's death, and Bougainville's circumnavigation of the world in 1766–1769.

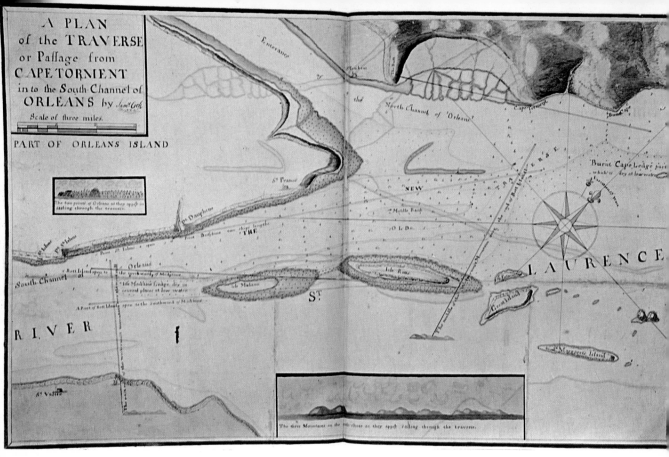

A PLAN
of the TRAVERSE
or Paſſage from
CAPE TORMENT
in to the South Channel of
ORLEANS by Jamͤ Cook

Scale of three miles.

PART OF ORLEANS ISLAND

Captain Cook in the Pacific

11

Left: this early example of the cartography work done by James Cook shows the traverse of the St. Lawrence River near Quebec. British warships followed this chart and more than 100 of them sailed safely up the river to begin the siege of the city of Quebec.

Below: Cook first became interested in the sea and worked with ships in Whitby, England. The little town on the coast of Yorkshire in northern England had a large shipbuilding trade. Given command of an expedition, Cook turned to Whitby to provide him with a ship, and the shipbuilders suggested the *Endeavour*. This watercolor shows Whitby harbor as Cook knew it in the mid-1700's.

James Cook, not quite the last, but indisputably the greatest of the Pacific explorers, finally solved the mystery of *Terra Australis*. By sailing south into Antarctic waters and accurately charting the coastline of Australia and New Zealand, he won a continent for Britain. He also proved conclusively that a Southern Continent extending from New Zealand to the Pole was non-existent. Then, having discovered the Sandwich Islands and accurately charted previous discoveries, he filled in most gaps on Pacific maps.

Cook was already 40 years old when he embarked on his first expedition to the South Seas. Son of a Scots-born farm laborer from Marton in Yorkshire, he had been apprenticed to a grocer and haberdasher and at 18 was apprenticed to John Walker, a Whitby shipowner. After several years' experience in an east-coast collier and other vessels, he volunteered in 1755 as an able seaman in the navy and was promoted to master's mate. During the Seven Years' War with France, Cook saw active service on H.M.S. *Eagle* and *Pembroke*, the former under Captain Hugh Palliser. Cook was present at the capture of Louisburg and the subsequent storming of Quebec. His charting of the St. Lawrence testified to his patience and skill as a marine surveyor, and he returned after the war to survey the coasts of Newfoundland and Labrador. It was Palliser, now governor of Newfoundland, who recommended him for his first command, of the schooner *Grenville*, and in the autumn of 1767 he brought his ship back from Newfoundland for the last time.

In 1768, King George III approved an expedition proposed by the Royal Society. Its destination was Tahiti and its official objective was to study the transit of the planet Venus, due to pass between the earth and the sun on June 3, 1769. Tahiti was chosen because it was in the area in which the transit could best be observed. The Society recommended the geographer and astronomer Alexander Dalrymple to lead the expedition. Dalrymple was one of the most dedicated and stubborn supporters of the *Terra Australis* theory, admitting it to be "the great Passion of my life," and had written, though not yet published, a book entitled *An Account of the Discoveries made in the South Pacific Ocean previous to 1764*. Although inaccurate in many details, the book marked the route of Torres from Espiritu Santo through the strait separating New Guinea and New Holland. But Dalrymple's seagoing experience was limited to short cruises through the East Indies in the service of the East India Company as

Above: James Cook (1728–1779) was one of the greatest navigators the world has ever known. He changed the vague map of a vast empty expanse of water into an accurate chart of much of the Pacific Ocean, with hundreds of tiny islands exactly located. Joseph Banks persuaded Cook to sit for this portrait by Nathaniel Dance in 1776, just before he left England on his final voyage.

Right: the *Endeavour* was originally named the *Earl of Pembroke*, and was used to carry coal to Scandinavia.

Far right: when the *Endeavour* was refitted for Cook, new cabins were built, the rig was replaced, the underplanking was reinforced to protect it from ship-worm, and it was armed with 22 guns.

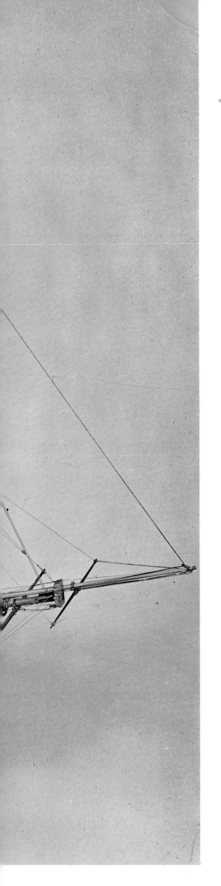

hydrographer, measuring and charting the ocean's waters. The Admiralty refused to consider him for the expedition. At this point it is probable that Palliser stepped in to recommend Cook. He was accepted, promoted to lieutenant and given command of the ship, a 368-ton Whitby collier named the *Endeavour*. She was "cat-built"— that is, with snub bows and deep waist—and only four years old, serviceable though not especially fast. Provisioned for 18 months, she carried 94 men on board, 71 officers and sailors, 12 marines, and 11 others, Among the last were the wealthy young Joseph Banks, a Fellow, later to become President, of the Royal Society and an ardent naturalist; two Swedish botanists, named Solander and Spöring; the astronomer Charles Green; and the artist Sydney Parkinson. Banks had contributed £10,000 (about $25,000) to the cost of scientific equipment. Among the crew members were five men who had served under Wallis.

Although the official destination was Tahiti, Cook carried secret instructions authorising him to continue south after concluding his astronomical observations in the hope of discovering "a continent

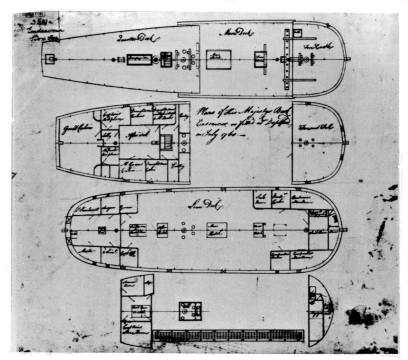

Left: the clear blue ocean, lush green vegetation, warm sunshine, and friendly atmosphere made Tahiti a favorite anchorage for the explorers. Today the island retains the image of a romantic South Sea paradise, and the tourist trade has become big business.

Right: voyages of exploration in the Pacific Ocean, showing the routes of explorers of the 1700's other than Captain Cook, the greatest of them all. They range from Roggeveen in the 1720's to Vancouver and Broughton in the 1790's.

or land of great extent." Should this not appear he was to sail south-west between latitudes 40° and 35° until he reached the eastern coast of Tasman's Staten Land (New Zealand). He could then return by either the Horn or the Cape of Good Hope.

The *Endeavour* was of course equipped with all the scientific necessities for the expedition's official duties, though surprisingly, Cook did not on this voyage take along the chronometer, which John Harrison had invented three years previously. He did, however, have at his elbow reference works, including selections from the logs of Wallis and Carteret, and an advance copy of Dalrymple's book, presented by the author to Banks. For the rest, Cook trusted to his good sense and navigational experience.

The *Endeavour* sailed from Plymouth on August 25, 1768, and after a smooth trip round the Horn entered the Pacific at the end of January, 1769. On April 11, Cook sighted the islands in the Society group and saw the peaks of Tahiti on the horizon. Two days later he anchored in Matavai Bay.

Cook and his men were greeted by the natives with shouts of "Taio, Taio!" meaning "Friend, Friend!" though Purea evidently no longer enjoyed her former authority. Tahiti proved a paradise for the

—— Roggeveen	1	1721-3
········ Bering (with Chirikov)	2a	1728-9
Bering (with Chirikov)	2b	1740-2
········ Byron (with Carteret)	3	1764-6
—— Wallis & Carteret	4	1766-8
Wallis	4A	1767

© Geographical Projects   140°

ARCTIC CIRCLE

Alaska

ST. LAWRENCE I.

BERING SEA

BERING I.
(KOMANDORSKIYE OSTROVA)

ALEUTIAN IS.

MT. ST. ELIAS

VANCOUVER I.

N O R T H

A M E R I C A

P A C I F I C

O C E A N

TROPIC OF CANCER

SANDWICH IS.
(HAWAIIAN IS.)

LINE ISLANDS

MARSHALL
ISLANDS

GILBERT
IS.

ELLICE
(TUVULU)
IS.

MARQUESAS

KING GEORGE
IS.

TUAMOTU

GALÁPAGOS
IS.

EQUATOR

SOUTH

AMERICA

OMON
ISLANDS
MALAITA SANTA
CRUZ IS.

WALLIS
IS.

SAMOA

SOCIETY IS.
TAHITI

NEW
HEBRIDES

FIJI

FRIENDLY IS.
(TONGA)

COOK
IS.

TUBUAI
IS.
(AUSTRAL IS.)

RAPA

PITCAIRN I.

EASTER I.

TROPIC OF CAPRICORN

NEW
ALEDONIA

JUAN
FERNÁNDEZ IS.

ASMAN

NEW
ZEALAND

DUSKY SD.

CHATHAM IS.

SEA

STR. OF MAGELLAN

— — —	Carteret	4B	1767
— — —	La Pérouse	5	1785–8
— — —	D'Entrecasteaux	6	
———	Vancouver & Broughton	7	1791–5
	Vancouver	7A	1791
	Broughton	7B	1791

Equatorial Scale

500   1000   1500   2000   2500
Miles

180°   140°   100°

naturalists, and Parkinson made sketches of landscapes, of the islanders in their canoes, and of local plants and animals. Cook's instructions to treat the population "with every imaginable humanity" were followed to the letter. Cook tried to regulate trade by forbidding the indiscriminate traffic in iron and cloth that had once purchased anything from a plump pig to an island maiden. Cook's journal skirts hurriedly over the latter aspect of Tahitian custom, though even he was bound to acknowledge the charms of their women. Despite a civil war, life seemed to have changed little. Two visits from Europeans appeared to have added shrewdness to the islanders' negotiating techniques. Solander lost his opera glasses, Banks a snuffbox, and Cook a pair of stockings while the three slept. The theft of a sentry's musket led to the offender being shot dead, the only unpleasant episode during the three months' stay.

June 3, the day on which they expected the transit of Venus, was clear and bright. The transit took place and the expedition took three sets of observations. In the weeks that followed, they sailed round the island, charting the coast and exploring the interior. Two deserters who had taken to the mountains with native girls were apprehended by islanders after Cook had reluctantly seized hostages. On July 13, the *Endeavour* sailed, together with Purea's companion Tupia, who proved invaluable as a pilot and interpreter, but who died when the ship reached Batavia. It was on Tupia's advice that Cook visited other neighboring islands, including Huahine, Raiatea, Tahaa, and Bora Bora. On the beach of Raiatea, Cook raised the flag and took possession of the entire group, naming them the Society Islands.

The historic part of the voyage lay ahead—the arrival at the end of that year off the coast of New Zealand, the circumnavigation of the two islands and the accurate charting of 2,400 miles of coastline, and the continuation of the voyage westward, bringing the ship to the eastern shores of the land then becoming known as Australia. These great exploits, the claiming of New South Wales for the Crown, and the passage through Torres Strait, close to the route followed by Torres, show what a brilliant navigator Cook was. On April 28, 1770, he made his famous landing at Botany Bay. When he finally returned to England, almost two years and eleven months after sailing, he found himself a hero. He himself minimized his achievement, writing to the secretary of the Admiralty: "Although

Above: Cook returned to Tahiti on his second voyage. His two ships anchored in Matavai Bay and Cook was instantly recognized by the Tahitians. They swarmed on board to embrace him and cover him with brightly-colored cloth.

I have failed in discovering the much talked of southern continent (which perhaps does not exist) . . . yet I am confident that no part of the failure of such discovery can be laid to my charge." And to his old friend and employer John Walker he wrote: "I have made no very great discoveries, yet I have explored more of the Great South Sea than all who have gone before me, and little remains now to be done."

Dalrymple and his school would not accept Cook's verdict on the Southern Continent. Dalrymple's second book, *Historical Collection of the Several Voyages and Discoveries in the South Pacific Ocean*, claimed that the continent had actually been seen and visited by Quiros. Even Cook could not positively say that there was no great land mass somewhere to the west of the southern tip of South America, for no man had sailed those waters. But he was prepared to lead another expedition, provided he could take two ships, in order to "put an end to all diversity of opinion about a matter so curious and important."

The Admiralty promoted him to commander and gave him the

Right: for islanders, the arrival of a European ship brought the excitement of bartering food and information for the strange new objects on the ship. Here a member of the *Endeavour* crew bargains with a Maori for a lobster.

Left: this set of cutlery was used by Captain James Cook on his voyages to the South Seas. Although forks had been in use since Saxon times they did not become widely used until the mid-1600's, and still had only 2 prongs.

Above: the *Resolution,* commanded by James Cook, was the first British ship to sail near Antarctica. When water became scarce ice was gathered and melted for drinking purposes.

462-ton *Resolution* and the 340-ton *Adventure*, the latter commanded by Tobias Furneaux, Wallis' second lieutenant on the *Dolphin*. Banks withdrew angrily from the expedition when Cook refused to accommodate his 15-strong party of scientists, artists, secretaries, and servants. Banks had wanted to take with him the celebrated painter John Zoffany, but Cook took instead a young artist named William Hodges. Two experienced astronomers, William Wales and William Bayly, proved of value, but the naturalist, a Prussian named Johann Reinhold Forster, was finicky and argumentative and neither he nor his son was a good sailor. On this voyage a chronometer made by Larcum Kendall was used to calculate the ship's longitude every day. In Cook's journals positions fixed by both latitude and longitude were accurately given for the first time.

The two ships sailed from Plymouth on July 13, 1772, and reached the Cape on October 30. Scurvy was kept at bay, but the enemies as they sailed south were intense cold and immense blocks of floating ice. On January 17, 1773, Cook wrote: "At $\frac{1}{4}$ past 11 o'clock we crossed the Antarctic Circle, and are undoubtedly the first and only ship that ever crossed that line." On February 8, the two ships lost each other in the fog. Cook continued on a southeast course but turned northeast on March 16 in the face of impenetrable ice. After 225 days at sea, and only one man ill with scurvy, the *Resolution* anchored at Dusky Sound on the coast of New Zealand's south island on March 26. Some weeks later they found the *Adventure* safely moored in Queen Charlotte Sound.

From New Zealand, Cook headed east, then north through the Tuamotu Islands and back to Matavai Bay (Tahiti). They received the customary warm welcome, though many familiar faces were gone. The naturalists and Hodges made the most of their month's visit and after touching at neighboring islands they sailed again on September 17. Cook took with him an islander from Bora Bora named Odiddy, and Furneaux took a Raiatean named Omai.

Continuing westward Cook passed the atoll of Manuae, which he named Hervey Island after one of the Lords of the Admiralty—part of a group later known as the Cook Islands—and on October 1 reached Eua (discovered by Tasman and named Middleburg). Here Cook was entertained by the "harmonious singing" of girls, and bravely sampled the intoxicating local beverage called *kava*. Next day they crossed to Tongatapu (Amsterdam) and were given pigs,

Below: after the cold and hardship of Antarctica the explorers were delighted to see Tahiti again. They arrived in time to see the Tahitians preparing for war with a neighboring island. Over 300 canoes took part, some as long as the *Resolution,* and nearly 8,000 men were needed to man them. This painting by Hodges gives an idea of the colorfulness of the scene.

Above: landing at Eromanga in the New Hebrides, Cook was greeted by a large crowd. They seemed friendly at first but suddenly tried to pull the white men's boat ashore. When the crew tried to stop them they threw arrows and spears. Cook ordered a volley of musket fire to drive the islanders back. Cook's record of non-violence was spoiled when several natives were killed and two of the crew injured.

chickens, fruit, and a copious supply of red feathers which the islanders greatly prized. Though the islanders were unabashed thieves, their behavior and appearance were so enchanting that Cook called their home the Friendly Islands—later to be known as Tonga.

Now they sailed for New Zealand. On the way the two ships were separated, this time for good. Cook was determined to explore the Pacific between New Zealand and Cape Horn, and left a message in a bottle for Furneaux advising him of his intentions. Battling through the ice, on January 30, 1774, they reached latitude 71° 10′, the farthest point south yet attained, only some 1,250 miles from the Pole. By now Cook was certain that no continent existed in these latitudes. "I will not say it was impossible anywhere to get farther to the South," he wrote, "but the attempting of it would have been a dangerous and rash enterprise and what I believe no man in my situation would have thought of . . . . I who had the ambition not only to go farther than any one had been before, but as far as it was possible for man to go, was not sorry at meeting with this interruption, as it in some measure relieved us, at least shortened the dangers and hardships inseparable with the navigation of the Southern polar regions."

Although it would have been simple to head for the Horn and home, Cook, warmly supported by his officers and men, decided to head north to look for more islands. For several days he was critically ill with a "bilious colic," but the devoted nursing of the ship's surgeon and the sacrifice of Johann Forster in handing over his pet dog to provide fresh meat and soup soon put him on his feet again. On March 12, they anchored off Easter Island, where Odiddy was able to understand the native dialect. Cook was not impressed by the flat, treeless landscape, nor did the statues greatly interest him. He and his companions saw none of the religious ceremonies described by Roggeveen, and because there was no food or water to be had they beat a retreat after four days.

Bound again for Tahiti, Cook plotted the exact position of the Marquesas Islands, the high islands discovered by Mendaña on his second voyage, and stayed for five days to take on water. Cook was greatly impressed by the islanders' natural grace. Many were as light skinned as Europeans. He described them as the finest race he had ever encountered in the South Seas.

By April 22, the sailors were back in Tahiti. The islanders were preparing for an invasion of the neighboring island of Moorea. Cook watched with wonder a mighty war fleet, consisting of hundreds of double canoes, manned by thousands of armed warriors, and decked with flags and streamers. He did not await the outcome, and on June 4 sailed for Espiritu Santo. Off one small coral island he narrowly missed being struck by a spear hurled by an islander and promptly named it Savage Island (Niue).

By mid-July the *Resolution* was among islands already discovered by Quiros and Bougainville. Others farther south were new. Cook

Right: Cook explored around Tierra del Fuego and saw many of the islanders in their huts. Almost every hut had a fire to try to ward off the cold. Christmas Day came while the ship lay off the coast of the island and the crew killed enough geese to provide one between three men. Madeira wine, which had improved on the voyage, was drunk in such quantity that most of the crew were sent ashore to recover.

William Bligh (1754–1817) was sailing master on Cook's second voyage around the world. On this voyage he discovered the breadfruit tree and was given the nickname "Breadfruit Bligh." In later years he became better known for the mutiny on his ship, the *Bounty*.

plotted the entire archipelago and gave the group the name New Hebrides. He left a detailed description of both the islands and their widely differing inhabitants. The Melanesians of Malekula, for example, he thought "the most ugly, ill-proportioned people I ever saw." Those on Eromanga were better looking but hostile. A third island, Tanna, was a beautiful place and the people spoke both Melanesian and Polynesian dialects, possessed flimsy outrigger canoes with lateen sails, and wore nothing save a belt and pieces of leaf. As for Espiritu Santo, Cook thoroughly endorsed Quiros' high opinion of the place. By now he was able to speak to the inhabitants in Tongan dialect.

In September, the *Resolution* sailed along the eastern coast of a mountainous land which resembled New South Wales so closely that Cook gave it the name of New Caledonia. It was, as he soon found, a large island whose people were friendly, intelligent, and, to his surprise, not thieves. Much of the land was barren but there were well tended fruit and vegetable plantations. Only lack of time prevented a survey of the west coast. As Cook remarked, he was regretfully compelled for the first time to leave a coast he had discovered before it had been fully explored.

On October 18, they anchored in Queen Charlotte Sound, to find that Furneaux had been there and removed Cook's message. The Maoris spoke evasively and confusingly of a shipwreck, and it later appeared that the *Adventure* had been involved in a clash in which some of the crew had been massacred. On November 11, Cook set off on a final attempt to find land in latitudes 54° or 55°. None was sighted. On December 17, they saw Cape Deseado at the western tip of South America, and spent Christmas in a cove off Tierra del Fuego. They made merry with goose pie and Madeira wine, and entertained dwarf-like local people who "stank of rancid oil." On December 28, they rounded the Horn into the South Atlantic, shattering for ever the myth of a Southern Continent. Cook did not disguise his relief, writing: "I was tired of these high latitudes where nothing is to be found but ice and thick fogs."

Anchoring in Table Bay on March 21, 1775, he found that Furneaux had preceded him by a year. On July 29, he dropped anchor at Spithead, England, after a voyage lasting 3 years and 18 days, having lost only four men, not one of them from scurvy. This had been due not only to a vigorous diet, which included fresh meat,

Above: during one of his visits to Tahiti, Cook was invited to see the ceremony of human sacrifice. This drawing by John Webber shows Cook standing to one side behind two boys flaying a pig. The priests, or *arioi,* are sitting in front of two men beating tall drums. In front of the priests is the sacrifice, a middleaged man of the lowest class who had been clubbed to death the day before. On the platform behind the grave diggers Cook estimated there were 49 skulls of earlier victims.

pickled vegetables, and scurvy grass (wild celery), but also to Cook's insistence on cleanliness and hygienic conditions, precautions that won him the Royal Society's Copley Medal, and a Fellowship.

Cook was now 46 and famous, and his account of his second voyage was as popular as, and much more accurate than, the garbled version of the first one written by a certain John Hawksworth. He was anxious to get back to sea but adamant in one thing. "I have now done with the Southern Pacific Continent," he wrote, "and flatter myself that no one will think that I have left it unexplored."

Right: everywhere he went Cook was fêted and invited to witness local ceremonies. Many of them were recorded in his journal and some were the subject of paintings by the artists on board his ship. This drawing by John Webber shows the dancing display put on by natives of Tonga.

On July 12, 1776, he sailed again in the *Resolution*, taking with him another Whitby collier, the 298-ton *Discovery*, commanded by Charles Clerke. First lieutenant of the *Resolution* was a veteran of the *Dolphin* and *Endeavour* expeditions, John Gore. Second lieutenant was James King, and the name of the master was William Bligh. Among the crew of the *Discovery* was a 19-year-old midshipman, George Vancouver.

On this occasion, Cook was bound for the still undiscovered Northwest Passage, approaching it from the land along the west coast of North America which Drake had claimed and named New Albion in 1579. Although England was at war with the United States, Benjamin Franklin, American minister in Paris, acknowledged the scientific importance of the expedition by instructing American vessels not to interfere with Cook's ships.

Traveling by way of the Cape of Good Hope, the ships were badly battered in the "roaring forties" and arrived at Adventure Bay in Van Diemen's Land on January 26, 1777, and at Queen Charlotte Sound on February 12. By the end of April they were back in the Friendly Islands, where they spent three months in pleasant but profitless

Above: when Cook arrived in Kauai, Hawaii, and noticed the similarities between these islanders and the Tahitians, he marveled at the courage that enabled the islanders to travel across the ocean in open canoes.

cruising. The Tongans put on boxing, wrestling, and dancing displays. The crew of the *Resolution* reciprocated with fireworks and marines' drills. On August 12, they anchored in Vaitepiha Bay, Tahiti. Here the western-style clothes and manners of Omai, the Raiatean youth who had been taken back to London by Furneaux, were much admired. So arrogant was Omai's behavior, however, that Cook was not sorry to land him at Huahine. Cook distributed cattle, sheep, goats, and pigs to the Tahitians, and amazed the natives with a display of horsemanship. He also attended, with some misgiving, a human sacrifice. After five weeks, during which the ship was refitted and Cook cured of rheumatism by a drastic but effective form of native massage, the expedition moved across to Moorea, Huahine, and Raiatea. Here there were three desertions from the *Discovery*, and the rearrested men were clapped in irons until they sailed. Then Cook turned his back for the last time on his beloved Society Islands and headed north on the most important and fateful part of the voyage.

Below: the king of Hawaii treated Cook like a god. The king himself was rowed out to greet the travelers and presented them with many gifts.

The expedition crossed the equator on December 22, and two days later they came upon a small atoll which they named Christmas Island. Then, at dawn on January 18, they sighted two islands. These proved to be the extreme western outposts of a group never seen before by Europeans. Cook named them the Sandwich Islands. They were later known as the Hawaiian Islands.

From one of them, Kauai, scores of islanders paddled out in canoes. They were darker than Tahitians but, amazingly, spoke a similar language. "How," wondered Cook, "shall we account for this nation's spreading itself so far over this vast ocean?" He was to be more astonished the following day when he found a safe anchorage. Hundreds of islanders prostrated themselves before him and rose only when he signalled them to do so. It was a reception fit

for a king or a god. In the ensuing weeks Cook found the inhabitants much to his liking. They were an "open, candid, active people," skilful at swimming, canoeing, and surf riding. They cultivated all the typical Polynesian fruits and vegetables and owned both pigs and poultry. Their huts, solidly constructed with hay and matting on the floor, were formed into compact villages. Their recreations included boxing and wrestling, though according to Cook, they were not as enthusiastic as the Tongans, nor was their music so varied and elaborate, the only instruments appearing to be drums. The women's dances were graceful.

The islanders were a handsome race, the men naked except for loincloths, and variously tattooed on their bodies and face. The women were beautiful, generally naked above the waist and no more

Above: it was this native club that knocked Captain Cook down, enabling angry Hawaiians to stab him to death.

Right: Cook was such a legendary figure that artists such as Zoffany painted romantic scenes showing his death. But the facts were far from romantic. James King tells of receiving "a small bundle wrapped in cloth" and finding it contained "a piece of human flesh, about nine or ten pounds weight . . . all that remained of the body" of Captain Cook.

modest in their attitude toward strangers than the women of Tahiti. Both men and women wore garlands of dried flowers or feathers round the neck and in the hair, as well as shell bracelets and necklaces. Although they had no weaving, their mats and bark clothes were expertly fashioned and their single outrigger canoes carefully constructed. In the Sandwich Islands only the paramount chiefs seemed to own double canoes. Weapons found on shore included spears, daggers, clubs, and slings. The islanders worshiped their gods on stone platforms which Cook called "marae."

When the *Resolution* arrived at Kamchatka Bay, Russia, after crossing the Bering Sea, the crew were entertained by the Russian colonists. Shortly before, in Hawaii, Captain Cook had been killed and the ship was now commanded by Captain Charles Clerke.

Cook's destination, however, was still New Albion, and by mid-February his ships had anchored in King George (Nootka) Sound on the west coast of what was later Vancouver Island. Here they saw their first Red Indians, hunters and fishermen who "had not the least pretension to be called handsome." They continued up the coast, crossing the Bering Strait. Cook stepped ashore briefly on the Asian mainland. Then they were among treacherous ice floes, across the Arctic Circle and reaching the farthest point north, latitude 70° 44', on August 18. Ice stretched to the horizon. Clearly it was suicidal to go on. At Unalaska in the Aleutian Islands they repaired the *Resolution*, finding the Eskimos "the most peaceful, inoffensive people." Then, to everybody's relief, they set sail again for the Sandwich Islands. On the morning of January 17, 1779, Cook stepped ashore at Kealakekua Bay, on Hawaii itself.

Some 800 canoes had surrounded the two ships, and now the islanders welcomed him as on Kauai, taking him for the reincarnation of Lono, God of harvests and happiness. Cook, though unaware of this, treated the chiefs and priests with due solemnity and consideration.

For some weeks all went well, but gradually Cook became aware of a subtle change. When he announced his departure, there was undisguised relief on the part of the chiefs. On February 4, they sailed, but a week later they were back after *Resolution's* foremast had been damaged in a gale. This time King Kaleiopu gave Cook a polite but frosty welcome. Relations with the islanders deteriorated and during the night of February 13 the *Discovery's* cutter was stolen. Next morning Cook strode ashore, escorted by 10 marines, and announced his intention of taking the king on board as hostage. At first the king did not protest but two other chiefs intervened and apparently changed his mind. He squatted on the beach, and soon a menacing crowd of Hawaiians, some of them armed, had collected. Word was then brought that a local chieftain had been shot and killed, at which the crowd closed in, throwing stones. The marines fought their way to the water's edge with musket butts and bayonets. Then Cook momentarily and fatally lost control, firing at an islander and killing him. The marines followed suit but the crowd rushed them, killing four and wounding others. The boats lying offshore also opened fire, despite Cook's calling out to them to stop. He turned his back to the islanders so that he could make his orders clearer, and stumbled. He was stabbed in the neck. Then the mob descended, clubbing and stabbing wildly. The surviving marines reached the boats but Cook's dismembered body was taken back to the village. A few days later, Clerke, now in command, received the pitiful remnants back from the now penitent and grieving islanders. It had been Cook's fate to be killed in as tragic and unnecessary a way as his famous predecessor Ferdinand Magellan had been.

Clerke did not live to see England, dying at sea after another futile attempt to find the Northwest Passage. It was Gore and King who brought the two ships home on October 6, 1780. The toll, at first glance, was light—seven men dead from illness, though not scurvy, three more from accidents, five more in the melée on the beach at Hawaii. But one of those had been Captain James Cook, and for him there was no replacement.

There was little left to discover in the Pacific after Cook had been there. But some gaps were still to be filled in, and some remarkable voyages to be made. The Frenchman Jean François de la Pérouse, in an expedition between 1785 and 1788, discovered Savaii, the largest island in the Samoa group. Two British captains sailed from New South Wales in 1788, and gave their names to new island groups—the Gilberts and the Marshalls. William Bligh won notoriety by commanding the 250-ton *Bounty*, detailed to take breadfruit trees from Tahiti to the West Indies in 1788. After discovering Bounty Island southeast of South Island, New Zealand, Bligh faced mutiny shortly after sailing from the Friendly Islands. The master's mate, Fletcher Christian, seized the ship and set Bligh and 18 companions adrift in the longboat. The *Bounty* sailed on to found a colony on Pitcairn Island, while Bligh navigated his frail craft through the Fiji and Banks groups and finally to Timor in a fantastic 12-weeks' voyage which took them more than 3,600 miles. Bligh went on to a distinguished naval career, eventually becoming governor of New South Wales.

Clerke's midshipman, George Vancouver, won fame for an expedition begun in 1791, which lasted four and a half years. He sailed by way of the Cape of Good Hope, Australia, and New Zealand, making valuable maps of the coasts. He discovered the Gulf of Georgia and surveyed the Pacific coast north of San Francisco for the first time. Vancouver Island, and cities in the state of

Although Cook had mapped much of the Pacific Ocean, his untimely death left some areas unknown. Jean François de la Pérouse of France (here second from right) led an expedition which spent part of its time filling in the details of the Samoan group of islands.

146

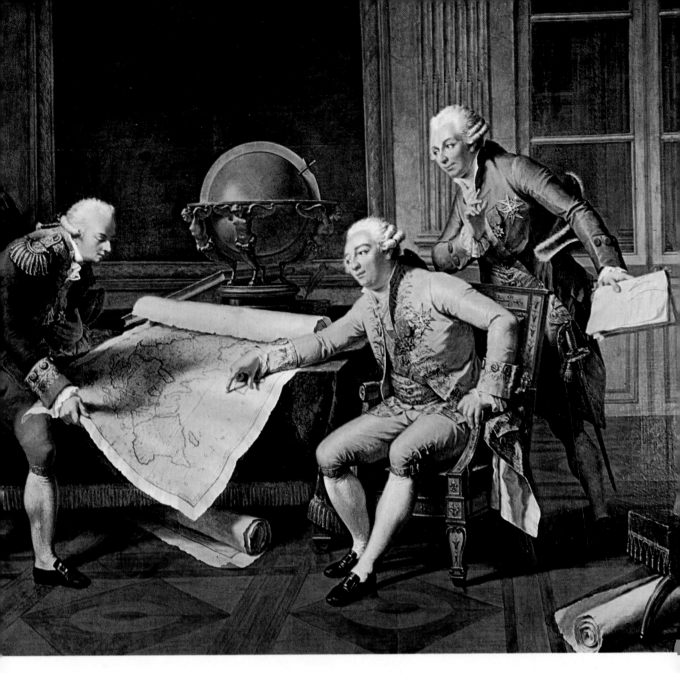

Washington and in British Columbia, Canada, are named for him.

Among many others who ventured into the Pacific, brief mention should be made of a number of men. The Frenchman Bruni d'Entrecasteaux made several discoveries in the Louisiade Archipelago in 1793. Fabian von Bellingshausen, commander of a Russian expedition, made discoveries in the Tuamotu and Fiji groups in 1820. Another Frenchman, Jules Sebastien César Dumont d'Urville, made a thorough survey of the Pacific between 1826 and 1828. And Charles Darwin, the English naturalist, participated in the famous surveying voyage of H.M.S. *Beagle* between 1831 and 1836, during which he visited South America, the Galápagos Islands, Tahiti, New Zealand, and Australia.

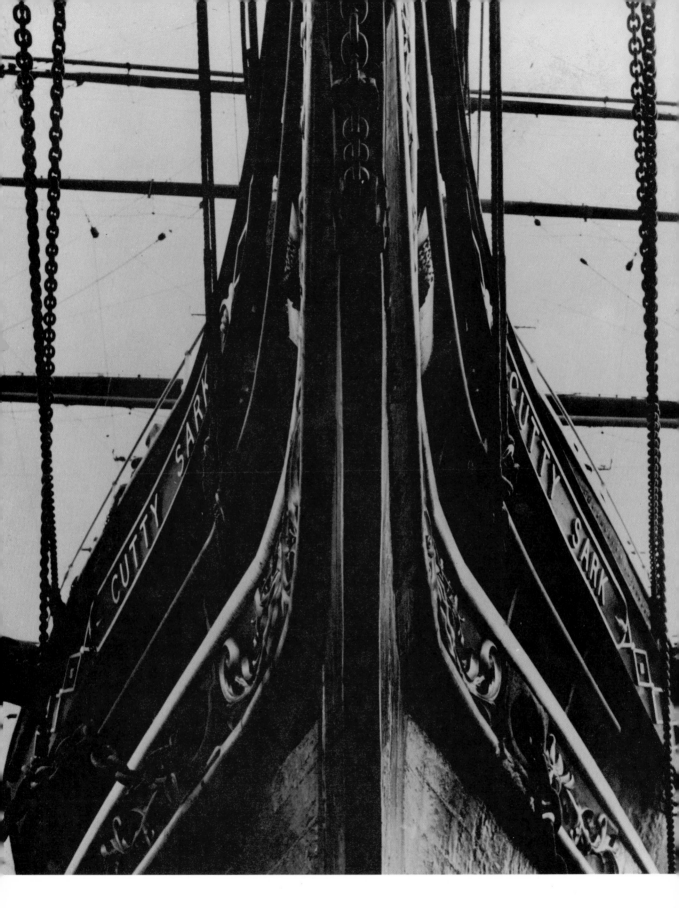

The Pacific Today

12

Left: the *Cutty Sark* sailed to and from
China by way of Sunda Strait and the
Cape of Good Hope. When sailing to
Australia, she went out by the Cape of
Good Hope and back by Cape Horn.

Two hundred and fifty years separated the voyages of Magellan and Cook. Gradually, the "civilized" powers of Europe had uncovered the secrets of the Pacific Islands. Two alien and contrasting cultures confronted each other. So far, contact had been limited and infrequent, providing no certain guide to future relationships. There had been instances of armed hostility, and examples of friendly cooperation. The choice lay with the newcomers and the governments whose interests they represented. Great opportunities beckoned if only policies could be tempered with wisdom and humanity. Yet there was grave risk of disaster if greed, prejudice, and ignorance were allowed to dictate attitudes and shape events. Would the next 100 years see adjustment or conflict?

History was quick to provide the unhappy and shameful answer. By the end of the 1800's, the worst elements of white colonialism had exacted a terrible toll on the Pacific Islands and their inhabitants. The record, of course, was not irredeemably bad. Not every European was a bloodthirsty villain, any more than all islanders were noble, peace-loving heroes. Yet, on balance, the material and spiritual benefits conferred on the island populations could hardly be justified in terms of the human misery left in their wake. Drink, disease, and firearms brought tragedy to the Pacific, and no amount of well-meaning missionary work or enlightened colonial rule could ever fully atone or erase the memory.

Right: one industry to profit from
exploration in the Pacific Ocean was
whaling. Now that the islands had been
charted, the whalers were able to use
ports close to the fishing grounds
where they could rest, and repair their
ships and equipment.

149

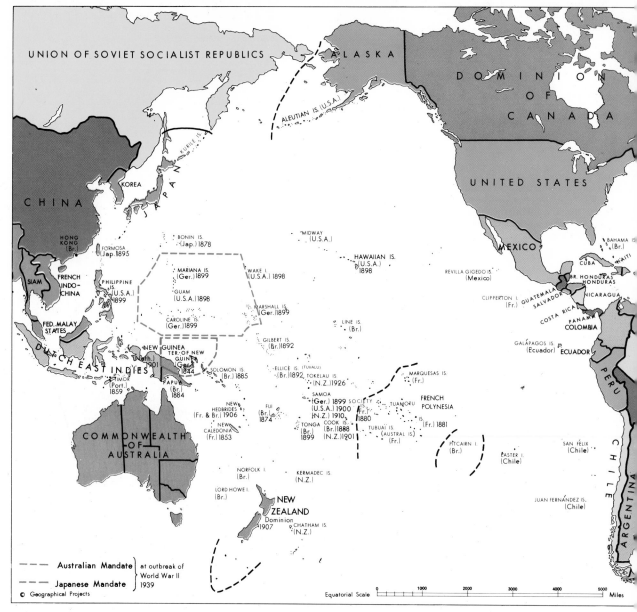

UNION OF SOVIET SOCIALIST REPUBLICS

ALASKA

DOMINION OF CANADA

ALEUTIAN IS. (U.S.A.)

KURILE IS.

JAPAN

KOREA

CHINA

UNITED STATES

HONG KONG (Br.)

FORMOSA (Jap.) 1895

BONIN IS. (Jap.) 1878

MIDWAY (U.S.A.)

HAWAIIAN IS. (U.S.A.) 1898

MEXICO

BAHAMA IS. (Br.)

CUBA

HAITI

SIAM

FRENCH INDO-CHINA

PHILIPPINE IS. (U.S.A.) 1899

MARIANA IS. (Ger.) 1899

GUAM (U.S.A.) 1898

WAKE I. (U.S.A.) 1898

REVILLA GIGEDO IS. (Mexico)

BR. HONDURAS HONDURAS

GUATEMALA SALVADOR NICARAGUA

CLIPPERTON I. (Fr.)

COSTA RICA

FED. MALAY STATES

CAROLINE IS. (Ger.) 1899

MARSHALL IS. (Ger.) 1899

LINE IS. (Br.)

PANAMA COLOMBIA

GALÁPAGOS IS. (Ecuador) ECUADOR

DUTCH EAST INDIES

NEW GUINEA (Neth.) 1901

TER. OF NEW GUINEA (Ger.) 1884

GILBERT IS. (Br.) 1892

TIMOR (Port.) 1859

PAPUA (Br.) 1884

SOLOMON IS. (Br.) 1885

ELLICE IS. (TUVALU) (Br.) 1892

TOKELAU IS. (N.Z.) 1926

MARQUESAS IS. (Fr.)

PERU

NEW HEBRIDES (Fr. & Br.) 1906

FIJI (Br.) 1874

SAMOA (Ger.) 1899 (U.S.A.) 1900 (N.Z.) 1910

SOCIETY IS. (Fr.) 1880

TUAMOTU

FRENCH POLYNESIA

NEW CALEDONIA (Fr.) 1853

TONGA (Br.) 1899

COOK IS. (Br.) 1888 (N.Z.) 1901

TUBUAI IS. (AUSTRAL IS.) (Fr.)

(Fr.) 1881

CHILE

COMMONWEALTH OF AUSTRALIA

PITCAIRN I. (Br.)

EASTER I. (Chile)

SAN FÉLIX (Chile)

NORFOLK I. (Br.)

KERMADEC IS. (N.Z.)

JUAN FERNÁNDEZ IS. (Chile)

LORD HOWE I. (Br.)

NEW ZEALAND Dominion 1907

CHATHAM IS. (N.Z.)

ARGENTINA

– – – Australian Mandate ⎫ at outbreak of
– – Japanese Mandate ⎬ World War II
© Geographical Projects ⎭ 1939

Equatorial Scale 0 1000 2000 3000 4000 5000 Miles

The commercial invasion of the Pacific began within decades of Cook's death. The traders—North American and British—were first in the field, eager to profit from the booming two-way trade with China. Chinese silks, brocades, tea, and porcelain commanded high prices in America and Europe. And the Pacific Islands yielded much that the Chinese coveted—pearls, tortoiseshell, *trepang* (the sea slug or sea cucumber, a rare delicacy), and sweet-smelling sandalwood. Then came the whalers, fishing the open seas from the Aleutians to the Antarctic. British, American, and French whaling vessels rivaled one another in their frenzied rush for oil and blubber, rapidly exhausting the fishing grounds. And in the off-season they would put into a small Pacific island harbor to refit, to take on provisions, to render and sell their oil, and to relax. What they had to offer in

Above: the Pacific at the outbreak of World War II in 1939. This map shows how the countries of the world had annexed the islands of the Pacific.

exchange for fruit, vegetables, and meat was far more interesting than the old-style knives and trinkets. They handed over rum and muskets. And they left behind something more deadly even than intoxicating liquor and bullets—disease. Venereal disease had already appeared in many islands as a result of the brief visits of early explorers. To this were now added measles, cholera, and the common cold, scourges which could only too easily reach epidemic proportion among a population lacking both immunity and protection.

Right: the Pacific Ocean offered new lands for Europeans to find and settle. Planters followed in the footsteps of explorers, establishing plantations and farms, like this one in New South Wales, Australia.

As time passed, the true potential of the Pacific Islands was recognized by the three major European powers of the day, Britain, France, and Germany. Australia and New Zealand were beginning to attract permanent settlers, and the smaller islands, too, held promise of much unexploited wealth. The mineral expectations proved disappointing in all but a handful of scattered sites, but the coconut, found virtually everywhere, provided a much needed industrial commodity—copra. On many a high volcanic isle the soil was fertile enough and the climate sufficiently varied to encourage the growth of food crops, coffee, cocoa, and, above all, sugar cane.

Soon the days of the itinerant whalers and independent traders were over. The missionaries moved in to convert the heathen. They dressed the islanders in western-style clothes and taught their children to read and write. The planters, many of them the children of early missionaries, arrived to claim the best land, negotiating with the islanders or forcing them out at gun point. Temporary trading posts became permanent settlements. Islands were taken under protection and later annexed. Sugar cane had been growing wild on some islands and planters discovered the stronger cultivated variety could also be grown. Labor was needed for the increasing number of plantations. Where it was inadequate locally,

Right: Captain Wilson was sent to the District of Matavai, Tahiti, in 1797 to start a mission. He is seen here with the king, queen, and chiefs of the district receiving what he thought was a freehold gift of the land. But it was meant as an expression of goodwill to the missionaries.

Below: among the men who came to the Pacific Islands were some of rare dedication and courage, like Father Damien, whose church at Kaluaaha in Hawaii is shown. His work among the ostracized lepers of the colony on the island of Molokai has remained a symbol of the good the outside world had to offer. Father Damien's work ended when he died of leprosy.

they imported workers, either from other islands or from the Asian mainland. The workers were often little better than slaves. This traffic was controlled by the so-called "blackbirders," whose brutal methods included wholesale kidnaping and murder. Often a native chief and his family would be seized by force and held as hostages until enough of the local inhabitants had signed a contract to work. Supposedly, they were to be given their passage home after having worked for a limited time. There were many employers who failed to fulfill this promise, and some who treated their forced labor so harshly that they died. Efforts were made by the British Admiralty to stop the practice, but many of the islands from which workers had been snatched were not under British control. It was not until 1904 that the Australian Government stepped in and finally stamped out blackbirding.

The cost of white domination was heavy. Epidemics, tribal wars, massacres, slave labor, alcoholism, and the confiscation of land from the island owners had depopulated islands and sown a harvest of bitterness and hatred. That it did not erupt in further violence and bloodshed was due to several factors. Among the more obvious negative reasons were powerlessness and lack of common purpose on the part of widely separated islanders. More positive and influential was a new sense of responsibility of colonial administrations, building on the foundations laid by early missionaries.

Left: an Ellice Islands woman washing dishes under a palm tree by the shores of the lagoon. Daily life for the Pacific islanders is often an incongruous mixture of newly-adopted materials and traditional patterns of behavior.

Above: tourism is a developing source of income for many of the islanders. Posters like this, particularly in distant places in the grip of winter, have proved a powerful lure to tourists tempted by sun and peaceful beaches.

After the London Missionary Society set foot for the first time on Tahiti in 1797, the trickle of Christian missionaries into the Pacific islands soon broadened to a steady flow. They came in the first place to convert, then stayed to provide medical care, and to educate. Much scorn has been heaped on the efforts of the missionaries—Protestants, Roman Catholics, Methodists, Mormons—who clothed native women in respectable "Mother Hubbards" and encouraged people to chant prayers and sing hymns in tongues they barely understood. In some places conversion was gradual and painless, elsewhere sudden and enforced. On the debit side was the substitution of an alien faith for a long-established pattern of belief and custom. Local cultures were destroyed, leaving boredom and bewilderment where there had once been warmth and meaning. To the missionaries' credit, however, were the continual, often successful battles against drunkenness, prostitution, and slave labor. They also greatly contributed to the disappearance of primitive practices such as cannibalism, the killing of infants, and ritual sacrifice. The preparatory work of the missions made possible the schools, hospitals, and other welfare services provided under the colonial rule of the 1900's. In some places it had led to complete political independence.

Today, only three major powers are in fact involved in the area—Britain, France, and the United States. Britain is only indirectly

Above: copra, which the Filipinos have harvested for generations, has become important to Western industry. Below: shell necklaces, made by the Papuans, are bought in their hundreds by tourists from all over the world.

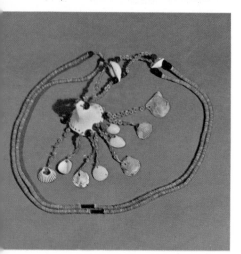

concerned in the fortunes of those territories administered by Australia and New Zealand. And, apart from the islands still controlled by other nations, there are a few that have retained or gained independence.

Fiji became an independent country in 1970. The Fiji group comprises some 350 islands, most of them small atolls, but some, such as Viti Levu or Great Fiji, are mountainous and fertile. Fiji suffered both from sandalwood traders, who stripped the forests bare, and from savage tribal wars, which were ended when the Wesleyans converted Chief Cakobau in 1854. The cotton shortage in Europe caused by the American Civil War attracted foreign planters who brought forced labor in from the New Hebrides and the Solomon Islands. This led to British annexation of the islands. The development of the sugar industry brought an influx of laborers from India, and Indians form a large proportion of today's population of about 537,000.

The Gilbert and Ellice Islands, included some of the Phoenix Islands and the northern Line Islands, and consisted mainly of atolls, with a mixture of Melanesian and Polynesian populations. They were

placed under British protection in 1892, becoming part of Britain's colonial empire in 1916. The Ellice Islands became independent as Tuvalu in 1978.

The Solomon Islands were a British Protectorate until 1978, apart from the two in the extreme north, Buka and Bougainville, which were administered by Australia. Once partially owned by Germany, the Solomons have suffered from a fickle climate, from disease, and from blackbirders. The islanders were shipped in their thousands to the coconut plantations of Fiji and the sugar fields of Queensland.

By the end of the 1880's, Britain had done much to bring slave labor to an end. In World War II the Japanese captured the Solomon Islands and there was bitter fighting on Guadalcanal and in the Coral Sea which separates the group from Australia. Copra now provides four-fifths of total exports. Copper has been found on Bougainville. But the islands have hardly lived up to the expectations of wealth implied in their naming.

Tiny Pitcairn Island, originally settled by Fletcher Christian and the *Bounty* mutineers, is a British colony administered from Wellington. The fate of the mutineers long remained a mystery. Ten of

Scenes like this Tahitian sunset have built up tourism, the island's largest industry. First painted by artists who sailed with explorers, and now photographed in color by the latest cameras, the islands have come to mean a romantic paradise on earth for many people in industrial towns and cities.

Above: Queen Liliuokalani (1838–1917) was the last monarch of Hawaii. She reigned for only two years until the monarchy was overthrown in 1893 and a republic established. The palace is still used by the state government.

Below: the European settlers brought more with them than trading goods and medicines. Barefoot New Caledonian women play a deft (if unorthodox) game of cricket under the tropical sun.

them were found in Tahiti and arrested. It was not until 1808, though, that the refuge of Fletcher Christian and the remaining crew of the *Bounty* was discovered. An American ship, the *Topaze,* chanced to call at Pitcairn Island. There they found a community of about 50 islanders, all part English, living contentedly under the rule of the last remaining survivor of Christian's followers. Later, attempts were made to move the population to other Pacific Islands where there was not such a great water shortage as there is on Pitcairn Island. The islanders returned to their home on each occasion, preferring to live there anyway. Today their descendants still live on what is one of the most isolated islands in the world.

The huge island of New Guinea, whose small population bears no relation to its area, has always been a divided land. Western New Guinea was once Dutch-controlled and has been administered by the Republic of Indonesia since 1963 under the name of Irian Barat or West Irian. Eastern New Guinea is now the independent country of Papua New Guinea. Until 1975 New Guinea and Papua were administered by Australia. The former, prior to World War I, was part of the German colonial empire, annexed by Bismarck in 1884 under the name Kaiser Wilhelmsland. It included the two northern Solomon Islands and the Bismarck Archipelago. Papua, which came under Australian control in 1906, also includes the islands of the Louisiade Archipelago and the Trobriand Islands, all producing little else beside coconuts.

New Guinea once attracted many traders to its coasts. They denuded the forests of sandalwood and ebony, and later came searching for gold. British policy during the 1800's was to pacify the primitive tribesmen, some of whom remained beyond their reach. As in other parts of Melanesia, head-hunting and cannibalism were practiced by many of the tribes of New Guinea. As late as 1957, 78 inhabitants of a village on the coast of southwest New Guinea were killed and eaten. Subsequent Australian administrations pursued an enlightened policy, paying particular attention to native welfare. Gold was mined in limited quantities, but lack of communications restricted economic growth.

The Bismarck Archipelago includes New Britain, New Ireland, and the Admiralty Islands, all now part of Papua New Guinea. Their economies depend on copra.

France has an important stake in the Pacific. The territories under her control comprise New Caledonia, Wallis and Futuna Islands and French Polynesia. New Caledonia, annexed in 1853, has proved the most valuable possession from the economic standpoint. From 1864 to 1897 the island of Nouville was used as a penal colony. Later, metal deposits were discovered and the island was developed for its rich deposits of nickel, chromium, cobalt, and other minerals. Though the nickel is fairly low-grade, it still accounts for four-fifths of the exports of the main island and the adjoining Loyalty Islands. Industrialization is well advanced in the port and capital of Nouméa. The population is mixed, a result of the introduction of

foreign labor over the decades, mainly Indonesians, Vietnamese, and islanders from the New Hebrides and the Wallis Islands.

The Society Islands—part of French Polynesia—include the large islands explored by Wallis, Cook, and Bougainville (Tahiti, Moorea, Huahine, Raiatea, etc.). The Tuamotu, Gambier, and Tubuai (Austral) groups, and the Marquesas Islands are closely associated with the Society Islands. Tahiti is mainly agricultural, with copra the foremost of many local crops. Here the London Missionary Society established its "missionary" kingdom under King Pomare II and his descendants. Yet it was the French who gained a lasting foothold after a punitive naval expedition sent to protest against the dismissal of two Catholic priests. When the last Tahitian king ceded his territory and abdicated in 1880, the island became a French republic. Papeete remains the administrative capital of the whole of French Polynesia, and Tahiti one of the most popular and exotic of all Pacific tourist islands. Many of the others are far off the tourist

The group of islands now called Samoa were once known as the "Navigators' Islands" because of the islanders' high standard of boatbuilding. Today the islands are divided. American Samoa is controlled by the United States, Western Samoa is independent. There are only 9 other independent islands: New Zealand, Nauru, Formosa, Tonga, Indonesia, Japan, the Philippines, Tuvalu (Ellice Islands) and the Solomons.

The Queen of England and the King of
Tonga caught in a brief shower during
Elizabeth II's tour of the Pacific. In 1970
the queen followed Cook's route on his
first voyage to the Pacific exactly 200
years before.

track. Among these, the Marquesa's Islands, in particular, have
been slow to recover from the unmerciful exploitation carried out
by the early European traders and whalers. Thousands died from
diseases taken to the islands by the Europeans, and whole villages
disappeared.

An unusual example of political cooperation is seen in the New
Hebrides, whose 12 main islands support a miscellaneous population of islanders, Melanesian and Polynesian immigrants, Europeans, Vietnamese, Chinese, and mixed races descended from the
first planters and laborers. The islands bore the full brunt of
European trading and whaling activities. Blackbirders cajoled and
forcibly removed the original inhabitants from the islands, and at
one stage a measles epidemic was deliberately introduced to reduce
the population. In these unpromising surroundings British interests
predominated until 1870, when the French staked a claim. Then, in
1906, an Anglo-French joint dominion was set up which has existed
ever since. Today the French element is very much the more
pronounced, and France takes 95 per cent of the islands' exports,
chiefly copra. In these islands, where the Pacific tragedy was once

Pearl Harbor in Hawaii is one of the largest and best-sheltered harbors in the world and the U.S. Navy has a large base there. In 1941 the harbor was crowded with ships when the Japanese launched a surprise attack. Eighteen ships were either sunk or damaged and there were nearly 4,000 casualties. Some of the ships are still in the harbor and serve as a reminder of the horrors of war.

enacted in full and terrible detail, the population is happily again on the increase.

The United States flag flies over many of the islands once occupied and developed under Japanese mandate. They include the naval bases of Guam and Wake Island, the Marshall, Caroline, and Mariana groups, American (or East) Samoa, and the Hawaiian Islands. Only Samoa and Hawaii have more than strategic importance. The six islands of East Samoa, with their capital Pago Pago, came under United States control under a convention of 1899 which divided the formerly independent kingdom of Samoa between the United States and Germany.

Hawaii had a very different and eventful history, its course decided by traders, whalers, planters, and missionaries. Once the islands supported a third of a million people, but a terrible cholera epidemic in 1804 brought about a sharp decline in numbers. By 1810, King Kamehameha I had conquered other local tribes and begun a wise reign. In 1840, Hawaii gained a written constitution. Britain intervened in 1843 to thwart a French occupation force, but it was American influence that predominated. A declining monarchy invited American protection, and a republic was proclaimed in 1894. Hawaii, too, was the indirect cause of American entry into World War II, when Japanese planes bombed Pearl Harbor in December, 1941. Because the Hawaiian Islands were 4,000 miles from Japan they were spared the ordeals of many of their southern neighbors in direct line of the Japanese advance. In 1959, Hawaii became the 50th State of the Union.

There are also a number of islands administered by New Zealand. These include the Tokelau (Union) and Cook groups, the latter exporting copra, citrus fruits, and tomatoes. A new constitution gave the Cook islanders control of their internal affairs in 1965. Nauru, important as a phosphate-producing island, was under Australian administration until 1968, and is now an independent republic. Easter Island, whose inhabitants were converted to Roman Catholicism in 1863–1864, was annexed by Chile in 1888. Western Samoa, part of the German colonial empire until Germany's defeat in World War I, became a New Zealand mandate within the Commonwealth, then a United Nations Trust Territory, and finally an independent nation in 1962.

Britain relinquished her rights in Samoa in exchange for concessions in the Solomon Islands and Tonga. There are more than 150 islands in the Tonga group. The capital, Nukualofa, is situated on the largest of them, Tongatapu. Here the Methodist missionaries won their most resounding success, abolishing heathenism in 1852, and ending the violent civil wars that had raged in the earlier part of the century. The chief, Tauga'ahau, had been converted earlier, ascending the throne as King George Tupou I, and ruling for almost 50 years. When he died in 1893, Tonga was a unified Christian kingdom, and his work was continued by his descendants. Previously under British protection, Tonga has now become

the only independent kingdom in the whole of the South Seas.

In spite of the excesses of colonialism, the results of the white man's impact on the islands have not been nearly so disastrous as might at one stage have been predicted. True, the Pacific "paradise" has become something very different. It is a western-style paradise, created by the bankers, the property owners, and the advertising men. There is profit in it for all concerned, for the businessmen shrewd enough to invest in it, for the shipping companies and airlines who serve it, for the tourists who enjoy it, and for the islanders who earn a living from it.

But nobody in the islands today need starve or want for medical attention. The birth rate continues to rise, the epidemics can be controlled, education is available to all. The fruits of civilization have come late to the Pacific Islands, and for many islanders the 1900's are still much like the centuries preceding. The Pacific area prides itself on being a melting pot of races, of traditions, of patterns of life—both indigenous and imported from abroad. There has not yet been time to see the shape of the future.

The islands of the Pacific Ocean are part of the modern world, and large cities have all the facilities and organization of international cities anywhere. Traffic moves briskly through the streets of Honolulu, skyscrapers are under construction, and business is efficient. But palm trees and men's brightly flowered shirts are visible reminders of the island's original atmosphere.

Left: an explorer holding an astrolabe, a navigational aid used until the 1700's for calculating latitude

Appendix

The vast Pacific spans more than a third of the earth's surface. To the explorers who first sailed there, its very immensity suggested the possibility of discoveries as boundless as the realms of imagination. This book has traced the gradual opening up of this huge area by men whose characters differed but who had one thing in common. Whether bent on piracy, on conversion, on commercial expansion, or scientific observation, they were all driven by a compelling spirit of adventure. As they struggled across a seemingly endless expanse of ocean, charting its scattered islands, they penetrated lands which had remained unchanged for hundreds of years. Their story is one, not only of courage and daring, but also of the first meeting between two worlds. Once that meeting had taken place, neither Europe nor the Pacific could ever be the same again.

No one can describe this dramatic epoch better than the men who were part of it. In order to give a wider picture of the Pacific explorers and their achievements, this appendix contains a selection of first-hand accounts of their voyages. Also included are contemporary documents which reveal something of the personalities of the explorers and discuss the implications of their discoveries.

For quick and easy reference to explorers mentioned in the text, the appendix also contains a section of short individual biographies, set out in alphabetical order. These are accompanied by maps to show the routes taken by explorers whose voyages were not mapped previously in this book.

Glossary, index, and credit information complete the appendix. The glossary gives a fuller explanation of terms used in the book and definitions of unusual or foreign words and phrases.

The Other Sea

In 1510, Vasco Núñez de Balboa became governor of the Spanish colony of Darien on the Isthmus of Panama. During the following three years, he led numerous exploring expeditions into the surrounding territory. In this extract from a letter requesting reinforcements, Balboa gives the King of Spain an account of the dangers and difficulties he encountered, and tells how he heard of "the other sea"—the Pacific Ocean.

Coat of arms of Balboa's monarchs, Ferdinand V and Isabella I. Their marriage united Castile and León (shown by castles and lions) with Aragon and Sicily (bars and eagles).

"Your most Royal Highness must know that after we came here, we were forced to travel from one place to another, by reason of the great scarcity, and it astonishes me how we could have endured such hardships. . . . I have taken care that none of my people shall go hence unless I myself go in front of them, whether it be by night or day, marching across rivers, through swamps and forests and over mountains. . . . Many times we have had to go a league, and two and three leagues, through swamps and water, stripped naked, with our clothes fastened on a shield upon our heads, and when we had come to the end of one swamp we have had to enter another, and to walk in this way from two or three to ten days. . . .

"At a distance of forty leagues from this city, there is a cacique [chief] named Comogre. . . . All the caciques and Indians of the country of Comogre tell me that there is . . . a great store of gold collected in lumps, in the houses of the caciques of the other sea. . . . They declare that there is much gold in very large grains in all the rivers of the other coast, and that the Indians of the other sea come to the residence of this cacique Comogre by a river, and bring gold from the mines to be melted, in very large grains and in great quantity. . . . I am told that the other sea is very good for canoe navigation, for that it is always smooth. . . . I believe that there are many islands in that sea (and) many large pearls. . . .

"It should not be forgotten that your most Royal Highness will be served by sending me reinforcements; when I will, if our Lord favours me, discover things so grand, and places where so much gold and such wealth may be had, that a great part of the world might be conquered with it. . . ."

Narrative of the Proceedings of Pedrarias Dávila *The Adelantado Pascual de Andagoya, trans. and ed. by Clements R. Markham. Haklyut Society (London: 1865) p. vi–xii.*

Balboa's Moment of Triumph

Balboa's plea for reinforcements met with no response. Instead he learned that his enemies had persuaded the king to replace him as governor of Darien. This news led him to undertake the greatest expedition of his career. On September 25, 1513, he became the first European to see the Pacific Ocean. Here, his moment of triumph is recorded by the chronicler Peter Martyr.

"A Quarequa guide showed him a peak from the summit of which the southern ocean is visible. Vasco looked longingly at it. He commanded a halt and went alone to scale the peak, being the first to reach its top. Kneeling upon the ground he raised his hands to and saluted the South Sea: according to his account he gave thanks to God and to all the saints for having reserved this glory for him, an ordinary man, devoid alike of experience and authority. Concluding his prayers in military fashion, he waved his hand to some of his companions, and showed them the object of their desires. Kneeling again, he prayed the Heavenly Mediator, and especially the Virgin Mother of God, to favour his expedition, and to allow him to explore the region that stretched below him. All his companions, shouting for joy, did likewise. Prouder than Hannibal showing Italy and the Alps to his soldiers, Vasco Núñez promised great riches to his men. 'Behold the much-desired ocean!'"

The Great Age of Discovery ed. by Arthur Percival Newton (University of London Press, Ltd.: 1932) p. 159.

Above: portrait of Balboa. After his discovery of the Pacific, Balboa was named *adelantado*, or governor, of the South Sea. But his triumph was short-lived. In 1519, he was charged with treason and beheaded.

Left: Balboa wades into the newly-discovered Pacific Ocean. In the presence of his men and his Indian guides, he claimed the sea and all the countries bordering it for Spain.

A New England in California

In May 1579, Francis Drake was edging his way up the northwest coast of America in search of the Northwest Passage At
the beginning of June, gales and intense cold forced him to
turn back and seek a safe harbor. On June 17, he anchored off
the coast of California. The following extract from notes kept
by members of his crew tells how Drake took possession of the
surrounding territory in the name of Queen Elizabeth, calling
it Nova (New) Albion, or New England.

"The newes of our being there, being spread through the Countrey,
the people that inhabited round about came downe, and amongst
them the King himselfe . . . with many other tall and warlike men. . . .
In the fore front was a man of goodly personage, who bare the
scepter, or mace before the King, whereupon hanged two crownes,
a lesse and a bigger, with three chaines of a marvelous length. . . .

"In comming towards our bulwarks and tents, the scepter
bearer began a song, observing his measures in a daunce . . . whom
the King with his Garde, and every degree of persons following,
did in like manner sing and daunce. . . . They made signes to our
General to sit downe, to whom the King, and divers others made
several orations, or rather supplications, that he would take their
province & kingdome into his hand, and became their King. . . .
In which, to perswade us the better, the king and the rest, with one

GILOLO IN.

Ternate   Tidore   Mutir   Machian   Bachian

Quam mirifice a Rege Moluccarum tubarū clangorem admirante, introvectus fuerit, delineatio..

Above: Drake's ship, the *Golden Hind* (originally called the *Pelican*), in which he sailed round the world. This illustration from a Dutch map of about 1595 shows the ship off Ternate in the Moluccas, where Drake took on cloves.

Left: the scene of Drake's coronation by the inhabitants of New Albion. As the crown of brightly colored feathers was placed on his head, the people shrieked, wept, and tore their cheeks with their fingernails in sacrifice.

consent, and with great reverence, joyfully singing a song, did set the crowne upon his head, inriched his necke with all their chaines, and offered unto him many other things, honoring him by the name HIOH, adding thereunto as it seemed, a signe of triumph: which thing our General thought not meete to reject, because he knew not what honour and profite it might be to our Countrey. Wherefore in the name, and to the use of her Majestie, he tooke the scepter, crowne and dignitie of the said Countrey into his hands. . . .

"Our General called this Countrey, NOVA ALBION, and that for two causes: the one in respect of the white bankes and cliffes, which lie towards the sea: and the other, because it might have some affinitie with our countrey in name, which sometimes was so called. . . .

"At our departure hence our General set up a monument of our being there . . . namely a plate, nailed upon a faire great poste, whereupon was ingraven her Majesties name, the day and yeere of our arrivall there, with the free giving up of the province and people into her Majesties hands, together with her highness picture and armes, in a peece of sixe pence of current English money under the plate, where under was also written the name of our General. . . ."

Sir Francis Drake's Voyage Around the World Henry R. Wagner *(John Howell: San Francisco, 1926) pp. 275–277.*

Drake Pursued

By the time Drake reached Nova Albion, his ship was laden with plunder from Spanish vessels and ports. Determined to capture him, the Spanish sailed after him. An English prisoner sailed with them praying they would fail. He was Miles Philips, who wrote this account of the hunt.

"When we were come to Acapulco we found that Captain Drake was departed from thence, more than a month before. . . . But yet our Captain Alcade de Corte there presently embarked himself. . . . We being embarked, kept our course, and ran southward towards Panama. . . . We met, at last, with other ships . . . of whom we were certainly informed that Captain Drake was clean gone off the coast . . . and so we returned back to Acapulco. . . .

"All the while that I was at sea with them, I was a glad man. For I hoped that if we met with Master Drake, we should all be taken: so that then I should have been freed out of that danger and misery wherein I lived, and should return to my own country of England again. But missing thereof . . . little doth any man know the sorrow and grief that inwardly I felt. . . .

"Our Captain made report to the Viceroy what he had done. . . . To which the Viceroy replied and said, Surely we shall have him shortly come into our hands, driven aland through necessity in some place or other. For he, being now in these Seas of Sur, it is not possible for him to get out of them again."

New Light on Drake *trans. and ed. by Zelia Nuttall. Hakluyt Society, Series II, No. 34 (London: 1914) pp. 225–226. Printed with the permission of Cambridge University Press.*

Left: back from his round-the-world voyage, Drake was knighted by Queen Elizabeth I on April 4, 1581, on board the *Golden Hind.* Despite Spanish requests for his punishment and restitution of the treasure he had plundered, Drake was richly rewarded for his expedition.

Hawkins Captured

Drake eluded the Spanish. But Sir Richard Hawkins did not. After a fierce battle off the north coast of Peru in July, 1594, Hawkins was defeated and taken prisoner. In the following extract from his journal, Hawkins records the scene at the height of battle and his impassioned refusal to surrender.

"The Spaniards with their great ordinance lay continually playing upon us, and now and then . . . invited us to surrender ourselves. . . . . The captaine of our shippe . . . seeing many of our people wounded and slaine . . . came unto me . . . saying, that if I thought it so meete, he and the rest were of opinion that we should put out a flagge of truce. . . . The great loss of blood had weakened me much. The torment of my wounds newly received, made me faint, and I laboured for life. . . . Yet grief and rage ministered force, and caused me to breake forth into this reprehension:

"Is the cause you fight for unjust? is the honour and love of your prince and countrey buried in the dust? your sweet lives, are they become loathsome unto you? will you exchange your liberty for thraldome? . . . can you content your selves to suffer my blood spilt before your eyes, and my life bereft in your presence, with the blood and lives of your deere brethren to be unrevenged? Is not an honourable death to be preferred before a miserable and slavish life? . . . Came we into the South sea to put out flags of truce? And left we our pleasant England, with all her contentments, with intention or purpose to avayle our selves of white ragges, and . . . to deliver ourselves for slaves into our enemies hands . . . ?"

The Observations of Sir Richard Hawkins, Knt. in His Voyage Into The South Sea *ed. by C. R. Drinkwater Bethune, Captain R.N. Hakluyt Society (London: 1847) pp. 207–210.*

The treasure galleons which plied between Spanish ports in South America were a favorite target for English attack in the 1500's and 1600's. Fierce naval battles were frequent during this age of corsairs.

Quiros and the King's Council

After his discovery of Espiritu Santo, Quiros' one desire was to return to the Pacific and convert the inhabitants of his "New World" to Christianity. Between 1607 and 1614, he made repeated proposals for a new voyage. Persistent, but not always tactful, Quiros sometimes allowed his sense of spiritual mission to cloud his judgment in dealing with court officials. In addition, adverse reports by some of his crew prejudiced his case. This extract from a report by the Council of State to the King of Spain gives an intriguing insight into official reaction to Quiros and his plans.

Above: the inhabitants of Big Bay, Espiritu Santo, where Quiros landed in May, 1606. Quiros instructed his crew not to ill-treat the natives, but fighting soon broke out between the islanders and the Spaniards.

"The Council . . . has thought fit to advise your Majesty:

"The Cardinal of Toledo . . . considers time spent on this matter time lost, for . . . your Majesty [has] neither the resources to keep even his present possessions, let alone new enterprises as remote and uncertain . . . but that, if your Majesty should later decide to undertake it, then it should be entrusted to a person possessing the character, prudence and reliability called for by such a project . . . for though Quiros has both knowledge and talent, other qualities are necessary to ensure success; and as leaving him out of it, and hence displeased, would be followed by difficulties, he could be told . . . that owing to the slender resources of the Royal Treasury no new enterprises can be undertaken for the present; and by using these arguments in friendly conversation, and doing him some favour here instead of in the Indies, he can be appeased . . . because if the enterprise were carried out with him there and had not been entrusted to him, then, should he feel himself aggrieved by this, he would become a source of mischief.

"The Constable of Castile . . . is fully in agreement with what the Cardinal has said. . . . The main care should be to prevent the inconvenience of Quiros placing himself, in discouragement, at the

Right: Quiros' memorial to Pope Clement VIII, requesting his support for a voyage of conversion to the Pacific. The Pope readily approved the enterprise and from then on Quiros was deeply convinced of the spiritual nature of his mission.

disposal of the King of England or other enemies.... It will be best if this man can be kept satisfied here ... but if he should insist on going to Peru, the viceroy should be sent a dispatch ... leaving the decision to him there after giving Quiros a very attentive hearing, and that the viceroy should be instructed ... by a further counter-dispatch to keep him there without giving him any permission, or coming to any decision with regard to him, except by your Majesty's express order; and it should be emphasized to him that this secret order is in no circumstances to come to the knowledge of Quiros. ...

"The Duke of Infantado: He considers this Captain Quiros to be an honest man with good intentions.... His [the Duke's] opinion is that it is not a substantial conquest, but that one of two things should be done: either to retain him here ... or to give him some dispatch with which he would go satisfied to Peru, but with the counter-dispatch mentioned by the Constable....

"The Count of Avila: He agreed with what had been said, adding that Quiros, knowing that his reputation stands low in Peru, will not go there willingly unless by official decision he has been already assured of the command of the enterprise, and this is not advisable; and so he should be kept waiting here ... or be dispatched as has been stated....

"The Cardinal, having heard the Council, added that he ... feared the despair and indignation of this man if he learnt of the counter-dispatch, and that he would approach other princes with his proposals. ...

"Your Majesty will command what should be observed and done in your best service."

La Austrialia del Espiritu Santo, Vol. II, *trans. and ed. by Celsus Kelly O.F.M. Hakluyt Society (Cambridge: 1966) pp. 360–365.*

The Painted Prince

When William Dampier returned to England after an adventurous 12-year journey around the world, he brought with him a colorful East Indian prince. Prince Jeoly, from the Serangani Islands off Mindanao in the Philippines, was covered with extraordinary tattoos. Dampier exhibited the prince in London, where this advertisement was circulated in 1691-1692.

"This famous PAINTED PRINCE is the just wonder of the Age, his whole Body (except Face, Hands, and Feet) is curiously and most exquisitely *painted* or *stained* full of Variety of Invention, with prodigious Art and Skill perform'd. In so much, that the antient and Noble Mystery of Painting or Staining upon Humane Bodies seems to be comprised in this one stately Piece. . . .

"The . . . admirable Back Parts afford us a Lively Representation of one quarter part of the World upon and betwixt his shoulders, where the Arctick and Tropick Circles center in the North Pole on his Neck. And all the other Lines, Circles and Characters are done in such exact Symmetry and Proportion that it is astonishing and surmounts all that has hitherto been seen of this kind. What Wisdom and antient Learning may lie veiled under those other curious Figures and mysterious Characters scattered up and down his Body, must be the Work of very ingenious Men to discover.

"The Paint itself is so durable, that nothing can wash it off, or deface the beauty of it: It is prepared from the Juice of a certain Herb, or Plant, peculiar to that Country, which they esteem infallible to preserve humane Bodies from the deadly poison or hurt of any venemous Creatures whatsoever. . . .

"This admirable Person is about the Age of Thirty, graceful and well-proportioned . . . extreamly modest and civil, neat and cleanly. . . .

"He is exposed to publick view every day . . . at his Lodgings at the Blew Boar's Head in Fleetstreet [London]. . . . But if any Persons of Quality, Gentlemen or Ladies, do desire to see this noble Person, at their own Houses, or any other convenient place, in or about this City of London: they are desired to send timely notice, and he will be ready to wait upon them in a Coach or Chair, any time they please to appoint. . . ."

Dampier's Voyages, Vol. I, *Captain William Dampier, ed. by John Masefield (E. Grant Richards: London, 1906) pp. 539-540.*

Above: tattooing is a common practice in many areas of the Pacific and particularly in the East Indies. The variety of designs is limitless. They are produced by puncturing the skin and rubbing in coloring matter.

Encounter at Easter Island

Jacob Roggeveen and his crew were the first Europeans to visit Easter Island and bring back information about its inhabitants. This extract from an account by Carl Friederich Behrens, an officer on one of Roggeveen's ships, the *Arend,* tells of the Dutchmen's first meeting with an Easter Islander.

"We stood in with our ships to look for a harbour, whereupon one of the natives came off in a small skiff to meet us. . . . We took him aboard our vessel and gave him a piece of linen cloth to wrap about his body, for he was quite naked; and we offered him beads and other trinkets, all of which he hung round his neck together with a dried fish. . . . He was of a brown tint, and had long ears which hung down as far as his shoulders. . . . We gave [him] a glass of wine to drink; but he only took it and tossed it into his eyes, whereat we were surprised. . . . We dressed our new guest in garments and put him on a hat, but he was evidently very ill at ease in clothing. . . . Our musicians treated him to a specimen of each one of their instruments; and whenever any person took him by the hand he began at once to caper and dance about. We were much pleased to see his enjoyment; but we did not come to an anchor that day, and therefore let him go back to the shore. . . . But he parted from us unwillingly . . . cast his glances towards the land, and began to cry out loudly in these words, *O dorroga! O dorroga!* . . . I make no doubt that . . . he was appealing to his god, as we could see great numbers of heathen idols erected on shore. . . ."

Behrens' Narrative of Roggeveen's Visit to Easter Island *from The Voyage of Captain Don Felipe Gonzalez to Easter Island, 1770–1, trans. and ed. by Bolton Glanvill Corney. Hakluyt Society (Cambridge: 1903) pp. 132–133.*

Above: an Easter Islander. This portrait, drawn in the 1770's, shows clearly the stretched ear lobes remarked on by the Dutch sailors. The pendant—a huge shell—is one of the islanders' favorite decorations.

Below: Part of a cast taken from a "rongo-rongo" tablet, showing the Easter Islanders' form of writing. Wooden tablets like this were used by priests when chanting ritual prayers.

Misery at Macassar

Limping into the harbor at Macassar on December 17, 1767, Carteret found to his dismay that the Dutch occupiers refused him permission to remain there. Carteret was desperate. He lacked provisions, his men were sick and his ship was leaking. He begged the Dutch to reconsider his position. The Governor of Macassar then sent two of his councilors on board Carteret's ship. This extract from their report and the Council's discussion of it show how the true facts of Carteret's plight led them to reverse their decision.

"The Captain . . . informed us most movingly of the pitiable situation which he undoubtedly was in. . . . He had now only a strength of 25 healthy men, officers included, as a result of the shortage of victuals and fresh water, and of the great discomforts they had endured in the course of the sixteen months of voyage, with steady storms accompanied by much cold weather. . . . The captain requested us to see the sick members of his crew, whom we found in a deplorable and lamentable state. . . . They were infected by scurvy to such a degree that the teeth of most men were loose or had fallen out; their gums were black and swollen and their legs as blue as lazuli. . . . The ship was very dirty inside and on the outside overgrown with grass, moss and shaggy vegetation. . . .

"The letter which you [the Governor] had sent with us had meanwhile on Carteret's request been translated . . . and when he had read it, we saw the unmistakable state of confusion and dejection into which he was thrown by your repeated order . . . to leave the harbour and these beaches and to go elsewhere. After a short silence he explained that he was not able to obey this order, since the misery of his crew, and their lack of all necessities, together with the bad state of the ship, certainly did not permit him to put to sea at this time of year, without exposing himself to the inevitable danger of perishing miserably with his whole crew. . . .

"This report was read [in the] Council and the Governor asked

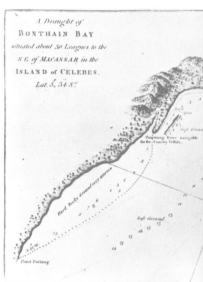

A Draught of BONTHAIN BAY situated about 30 Leagues to the S.E. of MACASSAR in the ISLAND of CELEBES. Lat. 5.34 S.

Left: Philip Carteret. His voyage was one of the most arduous in the history of circumnavigation. His ship, the *Swallow*, was not built for so long a journey and he met with constant misfortune and sickness. Despite his courageous completion of the voyage, he received little credit for his exploit.

Below: map of 1773, showing Bonthain Bay, southern Celebes, Indonesia. The Dutch allowed Carteret to go to this bay to repair his ship and rest his men. He stayed there for several months before returning home.

that close attention be given to the following main points:

"Firstly, the many emphatic orders of our Lords and Masters against the penetration of the English and other foreign European nations into the eastern governments. . . .

"But on the other hand . . . the extreme distress which this foreigner was in . . . and the question of how far one could and should, in a case like this, apply those orders. . . .

"Thirdly, the impossibility of his making for Batavia [present-day Jakarta] or any other coast to the west, in this westerly monsoon.

"Fourthly, the fact that, supposing we forced him to leave here in his present miserable condition, helpless and past recovery, his only recourse would be to set sail further to the east, to the spice regions, where he would be even less welcome. . . .

"Fifthly, considering that he was resolved to expose and surrender himself to all the bitter events and encounters that would befall him from our side; and that he was taking his ship further into the harbour, in spite of all refusals . . . and that the ship . . . without any shelter from the increasingly strong westerly winds, would run on a rock or beach; should we nevertheless stick to the resolution of this table of the 17th of this month. . . .

"And finally, could we justify such treatment, in these circumstances, before the Government of the Indies, or did not the tender dictates of reason and equity recommend help and compassion for this foreigner, as a Christian and a close ally? . . .

"When these main points had been considered . . . it was resolved unanimously to withdraw what had been decided on the 17th . . . and, on the contrary, to allow the captain to leave for the Bay of Bonthain, both for the repair of the ship under his command and for the recovery and refreshment of his sick men. . . ."

Carteret's Voyage Round the World 1766–1769, Vol. II, *ed. by Helen Wallis. Hakluyt Society (Cambridge: 1965) pp.375–381. Printed with the permission of Cambridge University Press.*

Stones Against Guns

With the arrival of Wallis came the Tahitians' first experience of gunfire. George Robertson, the _Dolphin's_ Master, speculates about their reactions to the outbreak of hostilities.

"They still behaved friendly until a large double canoe ... with several of the Principle Inhabitance in her ... was observed to hoist some signal ... the very instant that this signall was made all trade broke up, and in a few secants of time all our Decks was full of Great and small stones, and several of our men cut and Bruisd this was so sudden and unexpected ... that we was some time before we could find out the caus, therefor ordered the sentrys to fire amongst them, in hopes that would frighten them, but ... they all gave another shout and powered in the stones lyke hail amongst us which hurt a great many of our men, we then found lenity would not do, therefor applyed to the Great Guns and gave them a few round and Grape shot, which struck such terror amongs the poor unhapy croad that it would require the pen of Milton to describe. . . .

"While this skirmish lasted all the Bay and tops of the Hills round was full of Men, Women and children to behould the onset ... but ... when they came all running doun to receive their Victorious friends, how terrible must they be shockd, to see their nearest and dearest of friends Dead, and toar to peces in such a manner as I am certain they neaver beheald before—to attempt to say what this poor Ignorant creatures thought of us, would be taking more upon me than I am able to perform. . . ."

A Journal of the Second Voyage of H.M.S. Dolphin Round the World under the Command of Captain Wallis, R.N. in the years 1766, 1767 and 1768, by her Master, George Robertson _ed. by Hugh Carrington. Hakluyt Society (London: 1948) pp. 154–156._

Above: after the initial clash with the Tahitians, Wallis and his crew spent a wonderfully enjoyable time on the island. Wallis became a particular friend of the Queen of Tahiti. Here she is shown bidding him a tearful farewell as he leaves the island.

Left: the scene of the battle that followed Wallis' arrival off Tahiti. The double canoe which gave the islanders the signal to attack can be seen in the foreground. Unaware of the range of the _Dolphin's_ guns, the Tahitians at first thought they need only move a short distance to be out of danger. Some, however, preferred to swim to safety.

Tahitians, Beware!

With the return of Wallis and of Bougainville, news of Tahiti reached Europe. In France, it coincided with the theories of some philosophers about the desirability of a return to natural simplicity and innocence. In this extract from his writings, one of these philosophers, Denis Diderot, defends the right of the Tahitians to be left to enjoy their idyllic existence, and warns them of the dangers of future contact with Europeans.

"Ah! Monsieur de Bougainville, steer your vessel far, far away from the shores of these innocent and fortunate Tahitians. They are happy and you can only bring harm to their happiness. . . .

"You took possession of their country as if it did not belong to them. It is as unjust and senseless for you to write on your metal plaque, 'this country belongs to us' . . . as it would be for a Tahitian to land on our shores and carve on one of our mountains or one of our oaks, 'This country belongs to the inhabitants of Tahiti'. . . .

"No sooner had you appeared among them than they became thieves; no sooner had you set foot on their land than it was stained with blood. The Tahitian who greeted you with cries of 'Tayo! Friend! Friend!' was slain. . . . He gave you his fruits, his house, his wife, his daughter, and you killed him for a piece of glass which he took from you. . . . You and your men strolled about the entire island, Monsieur de Bougainville; you were welcomed everywhere; you enjoyed all its delights, and no one stood in your way. You found not a single door closed, for the use of doors is unknown. . . .

"At length you sailed away from Tahiti. These good and simple islanders bade you farewell. Oh! That you and your compatriots, and all the other inhabitants of Europe, might be engulfed in the depths of the ocean rather than see them again!

"As dawn broke and they saw that you were setting sail, they rushed forward, embraced you and wept.

"Weep, ill-fated Tahitians, weep! But weep for the arrival and not the departure of these ambitious, corrupt and wicked men. One day you will know them better. One day they will come, with crucifix in one hand and the dagger in the other to cut your throats or to force you to accept their customs and opinions; one day under their rule you will be almost as unhappy as they are. . . ."

Supplément au Voyage de Bougainville *Denis Diderot (Paris: 1796)*.

Denis Diderot (1713–1784), French philosopher and writer. He explored the moral implications of the discovery of Tahiti and was strongly in favor of what he saw as the natural simplicity of Tahitian life.

The Death of Captain Cook

When Cook and his crew awoke in Kealakekua Bay, Hawaii, on February 14, 1779, they found that the *Discovery's* cutter had been stolen. Cook decided to take the king of the island as a hostage until the cutter was returned. He went ashore, leaving orders that no canoe should be allowed out of the bay. The islanders implored the king not to go with Cook, and he finally abandoned his plan. A few minutes later Cook was dead. Lieutenant King wrote this account of the scene.

"Though the enterprize, which had carried Captain Cook on shore had now failed . . . his person did not appear to have been in the least danger, till an accident happened, which gave a fatal turn to the affair. The boats, which had been stationed across the bay, having fired at some canoes, that were attempting to get out, unfortunately had killed a Chief of the first rank. The news of his death arrived at the village where Captain Cook was, just as he had left the king. . . . The ferment it occasioned was very conspicuous. . . . The men put on their war-mats, and armed themselves with spears and stones. One of the natives, having in his hands a stone, and a long iron spike . . . came up to the Captain, flourishing his weapon, by way of defiance, and threatening to throw the stone. The Captain desired him to desist; but the man persisting in his insolence, he was at length provoked to fire a load of small-shot. The man having his mat on, which the shot were not able to penetrate, this had no other effect than to irritate and encourage them. Several stones were thrown at the marines; and one of the *Erees* [chiefs] attempted to stab Mr. Phillips. . . . Captain Cook now fired his second barrel . . . and killed one of the foremost of the natives. A general attack with stones immediately followed, which was answered by a discharge of musquetry from the marines and the people in the boats. The islanders . . . stood the fire with great firmness; and before the marines had time to reload, they broke in upon them with dreadful shouts and yells. What followed was a scene of the utmost horror and confusion.

"Four of the marines were cut off amongst the rocks in their retreat, and fell a sacrifice to the fury of the enemy; three more were dangerously wounded. . . . Our unfortunate Commander, the last time he was seen distinctly, was standing at the water's edge, and calling out to the boats to cease firing. . . . It is not improbable

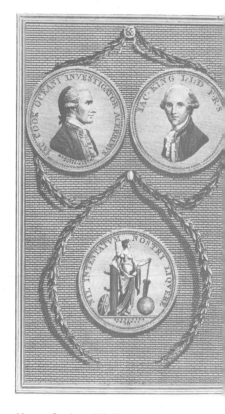

Above: Cook and his lieutenant, James King. One of Cook's favorite officers, King played a leading part in making a truce with the Hawaiians and recovering the remains of Cook's body for burial at sea. He later became commander of the *Discovery*.

Right: the *Resolution*. This 462-ton ship was used on Cook's second and third voyages. It was because of damage to her foremast during a gale that Cook decided to return to Kealakekua Bay, where he was killed.

that his humanity, on this occasion, proved fatal to him. For it was remarked, that whilst he faced the natives, none of them had offered him any violence, but that having turned about, to give his orders to the boats, he was stabbed in the back, and fell with his face into the water. On seeing him fall, the islanders set up a great shout, and his body was immediately dragged on shore and surrounded by the enemy, who snatching the dagger out of each other's hands, shewed a savage eagerness to have a share in his destruction."

A Voyage to the Pacific Ocean, Vol. III, *Captain James King (London: 1784) pp. 44-46.*

Difficulties and Discouragements

In September, 1795, the London Missionary Society was founded and immediately set about organizing a Christian mission to the South Seas. Among the missionaries sent by the society was John Davies, a Welsh schoolmaster. This extract from Davies' report of his work during the first six months of 1804 describes some of the "peculiar difficulties and very great discouragements" which the missionaries encountered.

"There was no way of collecting any number of children together. It was necessary to go to several places, or houses where they were; to take one here, another there, and two perhaps in a third place. They often refused to go, even 20 or 30 yards to meet with others, a circumstance which consumed much time, and materially diminished the utility of the exercise.

"To find [a] convenient time, was likewise no easy matter. After the novelty of the catechising was over, every little engagement was deemed an apology for neglecting it. Sometimes all were fishing, or they were in the mountains seeking plantains; at other times they were gathering breadfruit, or preparing their ovens, or else there was some diversion going on in the neighbourhood. . . .

"To obtain a suitable place was also extremely difficult. It was very rare to find the children alone, some of the old people being usually at hand. . . . They commonly kept up an incessant chattering among themselves, or with the children, so that often nothing could be done for noise and clamour. At other times, they would sit close to the children and whisper in their ears the most nonsensical

Above: the missionaries went first to Tahiti but gradually set up stations on other islands. They encouraged the islanders to build enclosed timber houses instead of open huts. They also developed a small export trade in local commodities, such as coconut oil.

Left: in the 1800's ships such as this brought many missionaries and traders into the Pacific. The islanders were eager for materials from Europe and America, but the missionaries would often supply the traders' needs from their own stores to prevent the islanders from obtaining firearms and alcohol. Far right: under the influence of the missionaries, the South Sea islanders adopted European clothes, shaved their hair, gave up music, dancing, and many of their traditional customs. Christianity began to take the place of local religions. The inevitable mixture of new beliefs with old is illustrated by this Solomon Island crucifix.

and ridiculous answers. . . .

"The wandering disposition of the young as well as the old, was also no small bar to their improvement. In Tahiti, every child capable of climbing an *Uru* [breadfruit tree] . . . is in a great measure independent of its parents, and wanders wherever it pleases. . . . Hence they rarely remained long enough in one place to learn anything to purpose. . . .

"Another difficulty was that both old and young had an idea the missionaries were their debtors, and ought to pay them for submitting to instruction. Instigated by their parents, the children used often to say . . . 'Give us pins, beads, and fish hooks, or else we will not be taught'. . . .

"Thus the missionaries continued their endeavours to make known to the inhabitants both old and young the great truths of the Christian religion, and some knowledge of these Doctrines did spread among the people, notwithstanding their indifference and inattention. Some of them wondered the miss. [missionaries] should give themselves so much trouble in travelling and speaking to them, and seemed to pity them for their folly. Others thought it was the custom of their country to do [so], and said one country had one set of customs, and another country another set of customs, and therefore let the *popaa* [the missionaries] have their own way; only they did not like to be troubled so often by them."

The History of the Tahitian Mission 1799–1830 *John Davies, ed. by C. W. Newbury. Hakluyt Society (Cambridge:1961) pp. 68–70.*

The Explorers

ANSON, LORD GEORGE
1697–1762   England
1740–1744: Sailed in command of six ships to attack the Spanish in South America. Captured Paita, northwest Peru. Rested at Tinian in the Mariana Islands. In his one remaining vessel, the *Centurion*, he sailed on to Macao, China. Set out again and captured a Spanish treasure galleon off Cape Espiritu Santo, Philippines. Returned to England via the Cape of Good Hope, completing circumnavigation of the world.
See map on page 181

ARELLANO, ALONSO DE
dates unknown   Spain
1564–1565: Captained the *San Lucas* on Legaspi's expedition to the Philippine Islands. His ship became separated from the others two weeks after leaving Spain, and reached the Philippines before them. Made the return voyage to North America in three months, touching the Mariana Islands. Returned to Acapulco, the first man to cross the Pacific from west to east.
See map on page 181

BALBOA, VASCO NÚÑEZ DE
1475–1519   Spain
1500–1501: Sailed west with Bastidas and settled in Hispaniola.
1510–1511: Stowed away on an expedition to the Isthmus of Panama. Helped develop the new colony of Darien and became its governor.
1513: Led an expedition across the isthmus and became the first European to sight the Pacific Ocean. Naming the ocean the "South Sea," he took formal possession of it for Spain. Remained for several weeks on the coast and visited Pearl Island.
1514–1516: Made a number of expeditions to the Pacific.
1519: Arrested by order of Pedrarias Dávila, who had replaced him as governor of Darien, condemned on a charge of treason, and beheaded.

BELLINGSHAUSEN, FABIAN GOTTLIEB VON
1778–1852   Estonia, Russia
1803: Took part in the first Russian circumnavigation of the world.
1819–1821: Sailed from Kronstadt in the Baltic in command of the *Vostock* and the *Mirnyi*. Went to Rio de Janeiro and South Georgia. Circumnavigated Antarctica and discovered Alexander I Island and Peter I Island, named for the czars. Crossed Antarctic Circle at various points. Cruised in the Pacific during the winter months, resting at Sydney and visiting Tahiti and many other Pacific Islands.

BLIGH, WILLIAM
1754–1817   England
1772–1775: Sailed as an officer on board the *Resolution* during Captain Cook's second voyage.
1787–1789: Commanded the *Bounty* on an expedition to take breadfruit trees from Pacific Islands for cultivation in the West Indies. Discovered Bounty Islands off southeast New Zealand. Following a mutiny near the Friendly Islands, Bligh was set adrift in an open boat with 18 of his men. Six weeks later, after a 3,600-mile voyage, he reached Timor in the East Indies.
1791: Introduced breadfruit into the West Indies.
See maps on pages 123 and 181

BOUGAINVILLE, LOUIS-ANTOINE DE
1729–1811   France
1756–1760: Served with Montcalm against the British in Canada.
1766–1769: Commanded France's first round-the-world expedition. Sailed to the Falkland Islands and on through the Strait of Magellan into the Pacific. Visited the Tuamotu Islands, Tahiti, and the Samoan group. Continued to the New Hebrides, where a strait is named for him. Sighted Great Barrier Reef. Discovered Bougainville, the largest of the Solomon Islands, the island of Choiseul, and the strait which separates them. Visited New Britain and New Ireland. Sailed on to Batavia and back to France.
1779: Fought in American Revolution.
See map on page 123

BYRON, JOHN
1723–1786   England
1740: Sailed as midshipman in one of Anson's ships, the *Wager*. Shipwrecked off the coast of Chile. Struggled back to England four years later.
1764–1766: Sailed round the world as captain of the *Dolphin*. Surveyed the Falkland Islands, and, unaware of the French presence there, claimed several capes and bays for England. Discovered Byron Island (Nikunau) in the Gilbert group.
See map on page 129

CANO, JUAN SEBASTIÁN DEL
(?)–1526   Spain
1519: Sailed with Magellan across the Pacific, as captain of the *Concepción*.
1521–1522: Became captain of the *Victoria* after Magellan's death. Sailed westward through the Indian Ocean. Rounded the Cape of Good Hope and sailed up the west coast of Africa in the one remaining vessel of the fleet.
1522: Returned to Spain, after the first circumnavigation of the world.
1525: Set out with Loyasa on an expedition to the Philippine Islands.
See map on page 69

CARSTENSZ, JAN
dates unknown   Holland
1623: Sent by Dutch East India Company to explore the north coast of Australia. During the voyage, the Gulf of Carpentaria and Arnhem Land were mapped. Cartensz was later killed by New Guinea natives.

CARTERET, PHILIP
1733–1796   England
1766–1769: Set out in command of the *Swallow* to accompany Wallis in his search for the Southern Continent. Separated from Wallis in the Strait of Magellan. Discovered Pitcairn Island and several islands of the Santa Cruz, Solomon, and Tuamotu groups. Explored St. George's Channel, which separates New Ireland and New Britain. Continuing to chart various small islands, he sailed on up to Mindanao, then south to Macassar. Remained for four months in Batavia to repair his ship. Returned to England

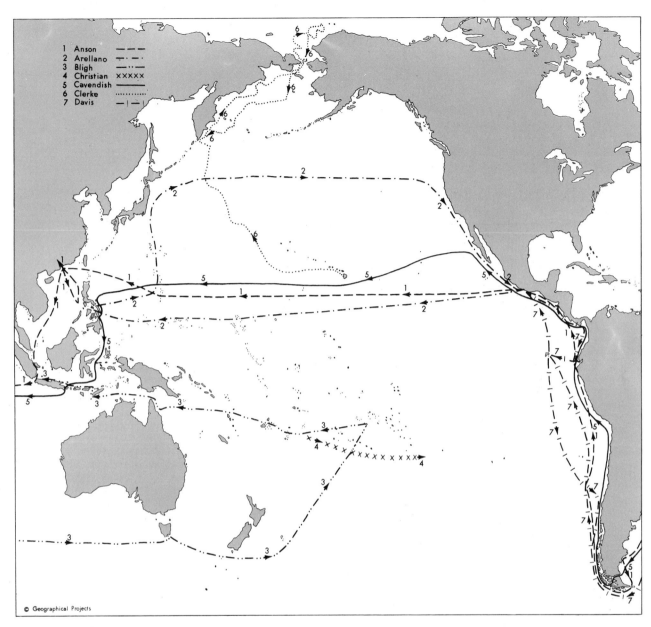

Key:
1 Anson   — — —
2 Arellano —·—·—
3 Bligh   ———
4 Christian ×××××
5 Cavendish ———
6 Clerke   ·········
7 Davis   —ı—ı—

© Geographical Projects

after a 31-month voyage round the
world.
See map on page 129

CAVENDISH, THOMAS

1555(?)–1592   England
1586: Set out with three vessels to
imitate Drake's voyage of circumnavigation. Reached Brazil and sailed
down to Argentina, where he
discovered Port Desire (Puerto
Deseado). Continued through Strait of
Magellan and carried out a number of
raids against Spanish ships and
settlements. Crossed the Pacific and
sailed for home by way of the
Philippine Islands, the Moluccas, Java,
and the Cape of Good Hope. Reached
England with his one remaining ship,

the *Desire*, having become the third
man to circumnavigate the globe.
1591: Commanded five vessels in an
attempt to reach the Pacific, but failed
to get through the Strait of Magellan.
Died during return journey.
See map above

CHENG HO

dates unknown   China
1405–1408: Led an expedition to
extend Chinese influence in the Indian
Ocean and South Sea. Visited Philippine
Islands, Brunei, Java, and Sumatra.
1408–1411: Reached Ceylon, whose
king he took prisoner.
1413–1424: Undertook four trading
expeditions to Malay countries.
1431–1434: Sailed to Persian Gulf.

CLERKE, CHARLES

1741–1779   England
1764–1766: Accompanied Byron in his
circumnavigation of the globe.
1768–1775: Sailed on Captain Cook's
first and second voyages.
1776–1779: Captained the *Discovery*
on Cook's third voyage. Became
commander of the expedition after
Cook's death in Hawaii. Continued the
voyage as it had been planned by
Cook, charting islands in the Sandwich
group and touching at Petropavlovsk,
in the Kamchatka Peninsula, Russia.
Sailed through the Bering Strait.
See map above

COOK, JAMES

1728–1779   England

1759: Charted St. Lawrence Channel from Quebec to the sea.
1762–1767: Carried out surveys of the coast of Newfoundland and Labrador.
1768–1771: Set out in the *Endeavour* to make astronomical observations and explore the South Pacific. Landed at Tahiti and observed the transit of Venus. Explored the Society Islands. Circumnavigated New Zealand, charted its coasts, and established that a strait separated the North and South islands. Mapped the east coast of Australia and took possession of it for Britain. Proved that New Guinea was not joined to Australia. Returned by Batavia and the Cape of Good Hope.
1772–1775: Commanded the *Resolution* and the *Adventure* on a voyage designed to establish or disprove the existence of the Southern Continent. Crossed the Antarctic Circle and sailed back to New Zealand. Sailed south again but was driven back by ice. Visited Easter Island, the Marquesa Islands, the Society Islands, and Friendly Islands. After resting at Tahiti, he sailed on to the New Hebrides. Discovered New Caledonia and Norfolk Island. Revisited New Zealand and undertook a final survey of the islands of Tierra del Fuego, and South Georgia. Sailed across the South Atlantic and back to England.
1776–1779: Set out in command of the *Resolution* and *Discovery* to search for the Northwest Passage from the Pacific to the Atlantic. Sailed to Tasmania, New Zealand, the Friendly and Society Islands. Discovered several islands in the Cook group. Revisited Tahiti. Discovered the Sandwich group, later renamed the Hawaiian Islands. Surveyed the Pacific coast of North America as far as Alaska. Discovered Nootka Sound, and Prince William Sound, Alaska. Sailed through the Bering Strait and struck northeast until stopped by ice. Returned to the Hawaiian Islands where he was killed on February 14, 1779.
See map on page 123

DAMPIER, WILLIAM
1651–1715   England
1680: Crossed the Isthmus of Panama with a party of buccaneers.
1680: Plundered coast of Peru and visited Juan Fernández Islands.
1684: Sailed with Davis in the *Batchelor's Delight* round Cape Horn and into the Pacific. Touched at Juan Fernández Islands and raided on the coasts of Peru and Chile. Continued to Galápagos Islands and Honduras.
1686–1688: Having joined with Swan in the *Cygnet*, set out from Mexico to cross the Pacific. Reached Guam in the Mariana Islands and went on to Mindanao in the Philippine Islands, where a mutiny took place and Swan was left. Dampier sailed on to Manila and China, cruised through the Spice Islands, and became the first English-man to set foot in Australia. Was marooned at his own request in the Nicobar Islands. From there he made a journey by canoe to Achin, Sumatra.
1689–1691: Made several voyages in the East Indies and returned to England.
1699–1701: Commanded the *Roebuck* on a voyage of discovery to Australia. Anchored in Shark Bay, Western Australia, and explored part of the coast, naming it Dampier Land. Refitted at Timor and sailed on to New Guinea. Discovered New Britain, and sailed through the strait separating it from New Guinea, giving it the name of Dampier Strait. Returned to Timor and set out for home. Was wrecked off the coast of Ascension Island. Rescued by a British ship.
1703–1707: Commanded unsuccessful expedition to Pacific.
1708–1711: Pilot on a highly profitable voyage of circumnavigation.
See map on page 69

DAVIS, EDWARD
dates unknown   England
1684: Took over *Batchelor's Delight* after the death of her captain. Sailed the Pacific, touching at Juan Fernández Islands. Made buccaneering raids on coasts of Peru and Chile. Visited Galápagos Islands and Mexico.
1685–1687: Sailed to Cocos Islands and Costa Rica. Cruised down South American coast to Guayaquil, Ecuador. Sighted an island in latitude 27°20' and named it Davis Land. This has never been rediscovered.
See map on page 181

DRAKE, SIR FRANCIS
1540(?)–1596   England
1567: Commanded the *Judith* on a pirate voyage to Spanish territory in South America.
1572: Carried out a number of raids in the West Indies. Crossed the Isthmus of Panama and saw the Pacific.
1577–1580: Sailed down the east coast of South America and through the Strait of Magellan. Proved that Tierra del Fuego is an island by discovering the strait now called Drake Strait. Continued up the coasts of Chile and Peru, plundering Spanish vessels and ports. Sailed on northward until forced back by bad weather. Landed on Californian coast naming it New Albion and claiming it for England. Having failed to find the Northwest Passage into the Atlantic, he sailed to the Philippine Islands, across the Indian Ocean and around the Cape of Good Hope. Returned to England, having completed the first English circum-navigation of the globe.
See map on page 69

ENTRECASTEAUX, JOSEPH ANTOINE BRUNI D'
1739–1793   France
1791–1793: Commanded an expedition sent in search of La Pérouse. Charted east coast of New Caledonia and parts of the south coast of Australia. Explored Tasmanian coastline, naming D'Entre-casteaux Channel, Bruny Island, and the entrance to the Huon and Derwent rivers. Died on way back to East Indies.
See map on page 129

GALLEGO, HERNAN
dates unknown   Spain
1567: Sailed from Peru as a pilot on Mendaña's expedition. With Ortega, discovered Malaita and Guadalcanal in the Solomon Islands.
For further details of voyage, see Mendaña de Neyra, Alvaro

GRIJALVA, HERNANDO DE
dates unknown   Spain
1537: Led an expedition from Peru into

the Pacific. Sighted several islands of the Gilbert group. He was murdered by his crew and his ship was finally wrecked off the coast of New Guinea.
See map on page 185

HARTOG, DIRK
dates unknown   Holland
1616: Sailed too far east on his voyage to Java in the *Eendracht* and touched on the west coast of Australia. Landed at Dirk Hartog Island. Explored Shark Bay.

HAWKINS, SIR RICHARD
1560(?)–1622   England
1593–1594: Set out to circumnavigate the world in the *Dainty*. Sighted the Falkland Islands, which he named Hawkins Maidenland. Plundered four Spanish vessels at Valparaiso, Chile, and overcame six more off Callao, Peru. Wounded and captured after a three-day battle with the Spanish off northern coast of Peru. Imprisoned at Lima.
1597: Transferred to Spain, where he remained a prisoner until 1602.
See map on page 185

JANSZ, WILLEM
1570–(?)   Holland
1605–1606: Sailed in the *Duyfken* along the south coast of New Guinea. Reached Cape York on the eastern tip of northern Australia. Sailed south into the Gulf of Carpentaria as far as Cape Keer-Weer.

KING, JAMES
1750–1784   England
1776: Sailed as lieutenant on Cook's third voyage. Took over command of *Discovery* after the death of Clerke. In company with the *Resolution*, completed the voyage back to England, where they arrived in 1780.
For further details, see Cook, James and Clerke, Charles

LA PÉROUSE, JEAN-FRANÇOIS DE
1741–1788   France
1785–1788: Set out to explore the Pacific coast of America and seek for the Northwest Passage. Reached Alaska. Visited the Hawaiian Islands. Discovered Necker Island, and sailed on toward

Asia. Reached Macao. Cruised through the Philippine Islands and on to Japan and Korea. Sailed to De Castries Bay, near present-day Vladivostok. Discovered La Pérouse Strait (now Soya Strait) between Sakhalin and the northern island of Japan. Rested at Petropavlovsk, Kamchatka Peninsula. Sailed on to Manua in the Samoan Islands, where some of his men were killed. Continued to the Friendly Islands and Norfolk Island. Reached Botany Bay, Australia. Probably shipwrecked in the Santa Cruz Islands, where remains of his vessel were found in 1827.
See map on page 129

LEGASPI, MIGUEL LOPEZ DE
1510(?)–1572   Spain
1564–1565: Led an expedition to the Philippine Islands. Founded a colony at Cebu and another at Manila. Returned to Mexico.
See map on page 185

LE MAIRE, JAKOB
1585–1616   Holland
1615: Sailed from Holland with Schouten, in command of the *Eendracht* and the *Hoorn*. Touched at Sierra Leone, West Africa, and sailed on to Patagonia. Discovered Strait of Le Maire between Tierra del Fuego and Staten Island. Leaving the strait and sailing southwestward, discovered Cape Horn. Crossed to Juan Fernández Islands and landed at islands in the Tuamotu and Friendly groups. Visited and named the Horn Islands. Sighted the east coast of New Ireland. Discovered islands in the Admiralty group, naming one of them for Schouten. Sailed on to Jacatra (present-day Jakarta), where the *Eendracht* was confiscated by the Dutch East India Company. Accused of infringing the Company's monopoly, Le Maire was sent back to Holland, but died on the way.
See map on page 69

LOYASA, GARCIA JOFRE DE
(?)–1526   Spain
1525–1526: Set out with del Cano in command of an expedition bound for the Philippines. All his ships were lost

before reaching Spain. He died at sea.

MAGELLAN, FERDINAND
1480(?)–1521   Portugal
1505: Sailed to India in the great armada of Francisco de Almeida.
1509: Sailed in the first Portuguese expedition to Malaya.
1511: Took part in Portuguese conquest of Malacca in Malaya.
1519: Set out, in the service of Spain, to find a westward route to India. After touching at Rio de Janeiro Bay, and stopping at several points along the east coast of South America, found the strait between Atlantic and Pacific. Sailed to the Philippines where he was killed by natives on Mactan Island.
See map on page 69

MENDAÑA DE NEYRA, ÁLVARO
1541–1595   Spain
1567: Led an expedition from Callao, Peru, in search of the Southern Continent. Sailed to the Ellice Islands (now Tuvalu). Discovered and explored the Solomon Islands. Continued through the Marshall and Gilbert groups and sighted Wake Island. Returned to Callao by way of California.
1595: Left Peru again, accompanied by Quiros, intending to colonize the Solomon Islands. Discovered the Marquesa Islands. Sailed on through the Ellice group. Discovered the Santa Cruz Islands, where he died.
See maps on pages 63 and 69

ORTEGA, PEDRO DE
dates unknown   Spain
See Gallego, Hernan

QUIROS, PEDRO FERNANDEZ DE
1565–1615   Portugal
1595–1596: Sailed for Spain as chief pilot on Mendaña's second expedition. Took command after Mendaña's death and went on to Manila. Left for South America in 1596 and reached Lima, Peru, in the next year.
1600: Went to Rome, where he obtained Pope Clement VIII's approval to his proposals for a new voyage of discovery and pledged himself to convert the inhabitants of the South Sea to Christianity.

1605: Sailed with Torres from Callao, Peru. Made discoveries in the Tuamotu Islands and in the Duff and Cook groups. Reached the New Hebrides and landed at Espiritu Santo, which he believed to be part of the Southern Continent. Stayed there for 36 days. Became separated from Torres, and sailed on toward Santa Cruz Islands. Returned to Acapulco, Mexico.
1607–1614: Went to Spain to petition the king for a new voyage.
1614: Left for Peru but died on voyage.
See maps on pages 63 and 69

ROGGEVEEN, JACOB
1659–1729   Holland
1721–1722: Sailed from Holland via Cape Horn into the Pacific. Touched at Juan Fernández Islands and went on to discover Easter Island. Sailed to the Tuamotu Islands, where one of his ships was wrecked. Sighted several islands in the Society and Samoa groups. Continued along the north coast of New Guinea, through the Moluccas to Batavia. Here the Dutch East India Company accused Roggeveen of infringing their monopoly and impounded his ships and confiscated his records. He and his officers were arrested and sent back to Holland.
See map on page 129

SAAVEDRA, ALVARO DE
(?)–1529   Spain
1527: Set out from Mexico on orders from Cortes to join Loyasa and trade with the Spice Islands. Sailed across the Pacific to the Moluccas. Found some survivors and attempted to return to North America.
1528: Left Moluccas again and skirted the northern coast of New Guinea.
1529: Sighted several islands in the Admiralty and Marshall groups and died at sea.
See map on page 69

SARMIENTO DE GAMBOA, PEDRO
1532–1590s(?)   Spain
1567–1569: Sailed from Peru with Mendaña. With Ortega, led scouting parties on Santa Ysabel, Solomon Islands, and was involved in fighting there. Separated from Mendaña on the return voyage and was arrested in

Mexico.
See also Mendaña de Neyra, Álvaro

SCHOUTEN, WILLEM
1567(?)–1625   Holland
See Le Maire, Jakob

SWAN, CHARLES
dates unknown   England
1683: Set out from England in the *Cygnet*, bound for the Pacific.
1684: Passed through the Strait of Magellan. Visited Mocha Island and Juan Fernández Islands. Plundered Spanish ships and ports. Joined by Dampier. Crossed the Pacific and was left ashore at Mindanao after a mutiny. Later joined with Davis in privateering ventures.
See also Dampier, Willian

TASMAN, ABEL JANSZOON
1603–1659   Holland
1642–1643: Sailed from Batavia to Mauritius with Visscher as chief pilot. Turned east and discovered Tasmania. Continuing eastward, he discovered New Zealand. Mistaking Cook Strait for a gulf, he presumed New Zealand to be a single island and sailed on to the Friendly Islands. Passed the Fiji Islands and continued to Batavia.
1644: Sailed again with Visscher from Batavia, along the southern coast of New Guinea and down to the Gulf of Carpentaria, North Australia. Established the continuity of the coastline from Cape York to Gascoyne River.
See map on page 69

TORRES, LUIS VAEZ DE
(?)–1613(?)   Spain
1605–1606: Sailed with Quiros from Callao, Peru. Became separated from Quiros at Espiritu Santo in the New Hebrides. Headed toward northern New Guinea but was driven back by gales to its southern coast. Discovered Torres Strait and proved New Guinea to be an island. Sailed on to the Moluccas.

URDANETA, ANDRES DE
dates unknown   Spain
1525: Was a member of del Cano and Loyasa's ill-fated expedition to the Philippine Islands.
1564–1565: Sailed again for the Philippine Islands on the *San Pedro* on

Legaspi's expedition. Returned to Mexico.
See map on page 185

VANCOUVER, GEORGE
1758–1798   England
1772–1780: Took part in Cook's second and third voyages.
1791–1792: Commanded an expedition to the northwest coast of America. Sailed to Australia and charted part of its southwest coast. Continued to New Zealand, where he explored Dusky Bay. Discovered Rapa in the Tubuai (Austral) Islands. Spent some time in Tahiti and the Hawaiian Islands. Reached California and sailed north, surveying the coast. Discovered Gulf of Georgia and circumnavigated Vancouver Island.
1793–1794: Returned twice to the Hawaiian Islands and continued his detailed exploration of the American coast. Reached Cook Inlet, Alaska, by way of Cherni and Kodiak Islands. Sighted Mount McKinley, the highest mountain in North America. On way home charted Cape St. Lucas, Lower California, and the Galápagos Islands.
See map on page 129

VILLALOBOS, RUY LOPEZ DE
dates unknown   Spain
1542: Left Mexico in command of six vessels. Reached the Philippine Islands but failed to complete return journey.
See map on page 185

VISSCHER, FRANS JACOBSZOON
dates unknown   Holland
See details of the voyages of Tasman, Abel Janszoon

WALLIS, SAMUEL
1728–1795   England
1766–1768: Set out with Carteret on a voyage of discovery to the Southern Continent. Sailed through the Strait of Magellan in the *Dolphin*, becoming separated from Carteret. Continued to the Tuamotu Islands. Discovered Tahiti, where he stayed for a month. Went on to discover the Wallis Islands. Sailed to Tinian in the Mariana Islands and back to England by way of Batavia.
See map on page 129

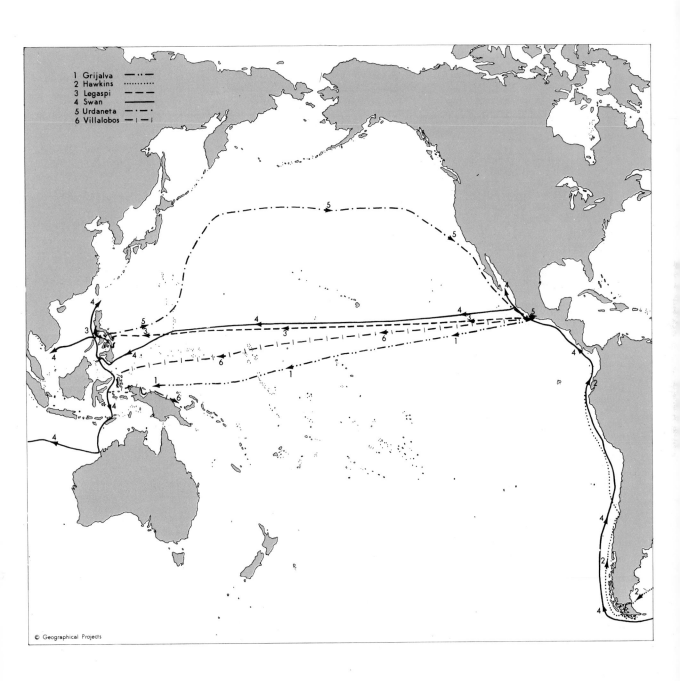

1 Grijalva   — ·· —
2 Hawkins   ·········
3 Legaspi   — — —
4 Swan   ————
5 Urdaneta   — · — ·
6 Villalobos   — ı — ı

© Geographical Projects

Glossary

anthropology: The scientific study of man. An anthropologist studies where the races of man originated, how they live, the languages they speak, and their ways of working, eating, courting, and worshiping.

arquebus: An early gun first used in the 1300's. Sometimes called a harquebus it consisted of a short metal tube attached to a wooden handle. It was loaded through the muzzle with black powder and a round bullet.

artifact: An archaeological term used to describe man-made objects, especially those of primitive man.

astrolabe: An instrument for measuring the altitude of heavenly bodies, from which latitude and time may be calculated.

atoll: A coral island. Usually a ring of coral covered with a thin layer of soil and tropical vegetation. The atoll encloses a shallow pool, or lagoon, which is connected to the sea by narrow channels on the windward side. Found chiefly in the Pacific Ocean.

blackbirder: A ship or person connected with the kidnaping of Pacific Islanders to work on plantations in Queensland and Fiji.

brigantine: Two-masted sailing ship which had square sails on the foremast and fore-and-aft sails on the mainmast.

cartography: The art of mapmaking, which dates back to the ancient Egyptians in the 1300's B.C.

cassava: A small shrub grown in warm regions. There are two kinds: bitter cassava, from which tapioca is made, and sweet cassava, which has edible roots.

chromium: A hard, grayish-white metal. Resistant to corrosion, it is widely used in industry.

Continental Drift: The theory that the continents were once part of a single supercontinent from which they gradually drifted away. The movement, caused by weaknesses in the earth's crust beneath the oceans, is thought to be continuing today.

copra: The dried meat of the coconut. It is valuable for its oil, which is used in soap and candles.

coral: The formation built up by millions of tiny animals called polyps. Individual polyps are only a fraction of an inch in size. They take calcium from the seawater and deposit it around themselves. Coral formations take on many different shapes, and colors. *See also polyp*

fossil: Remains or impressions of animals or plants which have been preserved in some way. Usually only the hard part of an animal (shell or bones) is preserved, when it has hardened and become stone, or when it has been buried in a material that hardened around it. Prints of thin objects, leaves or feathers, have been preserved when they became pressed into mud which has hardened. Rarely are whole plants or animals preserved as flesh and muscle decay quickly.

frigate: Originally a fast merchant ship that sailed the Mediterranean. Gradually the word came to mean a warship. Today a frigate is a warship of 2,000 tons or more.

galiot: A ship using both sails and oars as a propellant.

glacier: A river of ice and snow. It is formed when snowfall is heavy and piles up, compressing until it becomes a solid mass. The weight of the glacier will force it to move downhill at a rate of between a few inches and several feet a day.

lateen: A triangular-shaped sail hung from a long, tapered yard, or pole, that is suspended from the mast at an angle of 45 degrees. Ships with lateen sails found it easier to sail in light winds than square-rigged ships.

latitude: Helps to plot the position of a point on the earth's surface. It is a series of imaginary parallel lines, each drawn 1 degree or 69 statute miles apart, above and below the equator.

longitude: A series of lines running north and south and dividing the globe into 360 equal parts. Lines of longitude are measured from an imaginary line running through Greenwich, a borough of London, England, and generally thought to stand at 0 degrees longitude. Lines of longitude, together with lines of latitude, help us to plot our position on the globe. Longitude also helps us to know the time in other places, since an hour of time equals 15 degrees of longitude. Therefore when it is noon in Greenwich (0 degrees) it is 7 a.m. in New York (75 degrees west).

malaria: A serious, infectious disease. It usually occurs in tropical and sub-tropical countries and is spread by mosquitoes. A person suffering from malaria has intense attacks of chills, fever, sweats, and great weakness. For centuries quinine was used as treatment for the disease. Today new drugs have been developed but quinine is still used.

manganese: A hard, brittle metal, usually grayish-white in color. It resembles iron but is not magnetic.

monsoon: A yearly weather condition in India and southern Asia. During June and September strong winds blow from the southwest bringing with them heavy rains. The name was first used by Arabs for the seasonal winds which blow across the Arabian Sea.

nickel: A white metal. It is magnetic, takes a high polish and does not tarnish or rust. One pound of nickel can be drawn into a wire 80 miles long, or hammered into thin sheets.

outrigger: A canoe from the Indian and Pacific oceans, that has a log or a second canoe attached to a framework extending from one side.

This acts as a counter-balance, keeping the craft from capsizing.

phosphates: Chemical compounds which occur in rocks, the remains of animals, and the remains of plants. They are necessary to the growth of plants and animals and are used extensively as fertilizers.

pinnace: A small ship which usually sailed with a larger ship. It was fast and had two or three masts and a flat stern. In northern Europe a pinnace was used as either a warship or a merchant ship.

polyp: A very small creature that lives attached to the sea bottom. It resembles a hollow cylinder. The free end is a mouth, surrounded by a circle of tentacles which reach out for food. Coral is a compound form of polyp. *See also coral*

portolan charts: Charts used by sailors as an aid to navigation along the coasts of the Mediterranean. Drawn on sheepskin, they showed the outline of coasts and harbors and the location of shipping ports. The oldest examples of these charts date from about 1300.

proa: A swift sailing ship seen in the Pacific and Indian oceans. The weather side of a proa is rounded and the lee side is flat. Both the stem and the stern are alike and a small hull is attached to the main hull by poles to act as an outrigger. A large triangular sail propels the ship.

radiocarbon dating: A method of determining the age of an object by measuring the radioactive rays it gives off. A living man gives off 918 radioactive rays an hour. After death his body loses half its radioactivity in the first 5,750 years and half the remainder each following 5,750 years. Therefore a skull giving off 229 rays every hour would be 11,500 years old, whereas a skull giving off only 3 rays per hour would be 46,000 years old.

Royal Society: The oldest scientific society in the world. As early as 1645 London scientists were holding weekly meetings. In 1660, the society was recognized by King Charles II of England and was organized under the title *The Royal Society of London for Improving Natural Knowledge.* Over the years the society has directed expeditions and helped with scientific teaching in schools. In 1752, the society was responsible for correcting the calendar and later for improving the protection of ships from lightning. It also perfected the methods used for measuring latitude.

scurvy: A disease resulting from a lack of vitamin C in the diet, which was once common among sailors. Wounds do not heal properly and the person bruises easily. The walls of capillaries become weak and slight pressure causes them to break. The mouth and gums become sore, the gums bleed and the teeth become loose. The person's joints become sore, he loses his appetite and becomes restless. Food containing vitamin C, such as citrus fruits, tomatoes, cabbage, lettuce, celery, onions, carrots and potatoes—eaten fresh— can prevent and sometimes help to cure scurvy.

scuttle: To destroy a vessel by cutting holes in its sides, deck, and bottom so that it sinks.

stele: A pillar or slab of any kind of metal or stone set up in commemoration of an event or a person. They are sometimes decorated and usually inscribed.

tabu (tapu, or taboo): A Polynesian word meaning to forbid or exclude. Certain objects were set apart as sacred, unclean or harmful and people were forbidden to touch them. Burial grounds, sick people, foreigners, parts of a person's body, and things belonging to a chief or priest might be tabu.

taro: A tropical plant grown mainly in Hawaii and other Pacific Islands. It has a large underground stem which can be eaten and which forms a large part of the diet of many Pacific Islanders.

trade wind: A strong wind that blows toward the equator from the northeast or southeast. These winds follow a regular path and were given the name "trade wind" by early navigators. Sailing ships, and the men who sailed them, depended on the trade winds as their main means of traveling the shortest distance from one place to another.

Treaty of Tordesillas: Treaty of 1494 concerning the rights of Spain and Portugal to newly-discovered lands. In 1493, Pope Alexander VI drew an imaginary line from north to south, about 340 miles west of the Azores and Cape Verde Islands. He decreed that Spain should have the right to claim lands lying to the west of the line and Portugal land to the east of it. This proved unsatisfactory to both countries and in 1494, by the Treaty of Tordesillas, they agreed to move the line to about 1,250 miles west of the Cape Verde Islands. The exact position of the line has never been determined but it is generally thought to have been situated near the 48° west longitude line.

Index

Picture Credits

Listed below are the sources of all the illustrations in this book. To identify the source of a particular illustration, first find the relevant page on the diagram opposite. The number in black in the appropriate position on that page refers to the credit as listed below.

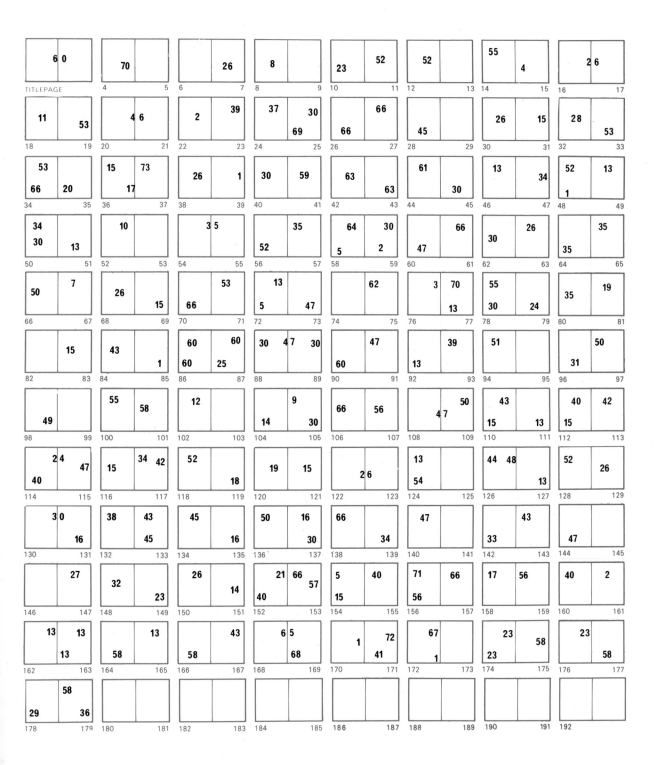